MAKING PEACE

MAKING PEACE

A Guide to Overcoming
Church Conflict

JIM VAN YPEREN

For Sharon
Together

Blessed are the peacemakers,
for they will be called sons of God.

Matthew 5:9

But he was pierced for our transgressions,
he was crushed for our iniquities;
the punishment that brought us peace was upon him,
and by his wounds we are healed.

Isaiah 53:5

For he himself is our peace, who has
made the two one and has destroyed
the barrier, the dividing wall of hostility.

Ephesians 2:14

Make every effort to keep the unity of
the Spirit through the bond of peace.

Ephesians 4:3

For the kingdom of God
is not a matter of eating and drinking,
but of righteousness, peace and joy
in the Holy Spirit.

Romans 14:17

CONTENTS

ACKNOWLEDGMENTS

This book is possible through the support and encouragement of many people. First and foremost I thank my wife, Sharon, and our children, Nate and Sarah, who joined me in the spiritual discovery of speaking the truth in love and in growing redemptive community. Their sacrifice, patience, and love for me is a treasured gift.

I am grateful to the founding board of Metanoia Ministries: Jim Bowen, Dave Brooks, Richard Bush, Darin Chin, David Fitch, Larry Keillor, Terri Noordmans, and John Ryser. They gave me the mandate and the freedom to complete this manuscript. Special thanks are due to David Fitch for helping shape my understanding of theology and biblical community during the past decade, and to John Soper, whose partnership in ministry during the past five years provided the platform to develop and refine the peacemaking principles in this book.

I am particularly grateful to our staff, Luanne Barker and Matt Brubaker, for their encouragement, proofreading, and for carrying on the ministry in my absence.

Finally, I am grateful to Elaine James, who provided early edit-ing advice for the manuscript, and to Jim Bell and Jim Vincent of Moody Press, who guided this book to publication.

INTRODUCTION

It was Sunday morning, the day after our report of findings to First Church. I was making my way to the pulpit to give announcements and welcome visitors to morning worship.

I had been the intentional interim pastor for six weeks already, spending ten hours a day, three days a week interviewing 209 current and former members. The findings were alarming.

First Church was in deep crisis. Attendance had dropped from five hundred to less than two hundred. In addition to interviewing current members, I had sent a letter to 119 families who had left the church in the past three years, asking them to tell me their story. Ninety-six people wrote back. Most sent multipage letters stapled to their survey. Story after story recounted anger, pain, and sorrow from unreconciled wounds. For most, this was the first contact from the church since they had left—months or years before.

The night before I had asked the entire governing board to resign and for the church to be placed on emergency rehabilitation status under the direction of the denomination. It was now my task to lead the church through the process of confronting, confessing, and reconciling the conflict.

I made my way to the lectern with two concerns: first, that the church face the crisis honestly and directly, and, second, to see the coming weeks as an opportunity to see God work.

The congregation was buzzing with handshakes and whispers. A few latecomers found their seats, and several parents hushed their children. "We welcome you to our worship service this morning," I began. "We are glad you are here." Most lifted their heads when they heard me say: "And we offer a special welcome to those of you who may be visiting with us for the first time. You need to know that this is a sick church."

With those words, all the normal fidgeting and paper shuffling that goes on during announcements came to an abrupt halt. The sanctuary became stone quiet. People wondered if they had heard me correctly. *Did he say sick?* I paused, then continued.

"The good news is that we know we are sick and that we are determined to change. So we invite you to come back over the following weeks and see what God is going to do in our midst."

After the service, two of the former elders made a straight line toward me. Both were offended and angry at my announcement.

"Why?" I asked. "It is a true statement. We are a sick church."

This flustered them because they thought their reasons were obvious. "Every church has problems," one man said. "We are not that much worse than others." "There is no perfect church," the other elder reminded me. We talked about their concerns and, having heard their point, I agreed that the word "sick" should not be used again. (The next week I said the church was "not healthy.")

In the intervening months, God was gracious to reconcile past conflicts and set this church on a course of restoration. After six months, my work was done, and it was time for me to leave.

When I completed my final report to the congregation, a couple came up to me and said, "We want you to know that the first Sunday we visited here was the day you said, 'This is a sick church' from the pulpit. We could not believe you said that. We had been in a lot of sick churches before. This was the only place we heard a pastor admit it publicly. We knew we had to stay—just to see what God was going to do."

When church leaders and members are willing to honestly accept, openly confess, and intentionally address the underlying causes of church conflict, God will repair and restore the church. It starts with being truthful about current reality—with admitting we are sick. In the pages that follow you will learn why churches become unhealthy and how God wants to heal them so they may become thriving communities of faith.

You may be facing some level of conflict in your church or your life right now. Whatever your situation—private or public—and whoever you are—pastor or lay leader—the church is the place God would have you reconcile.

This book collects the lessons and experiences of more than ten years' work in church-conflict reconciliation. In that time, the ministry my wife and I founded—Metanoia Ministries—has conducted more than two dozen church assessments of congregations in deep conflict. Each church we served received a comprehensive evaluation involving from twelve weeks to two years of reconciliation work. These churches represent eleven different denominations, with weekly attendance from one hundred to fifteen hundred people.

During this period I also served five deeply conflicted churches as an "intentional interim pastor." An intentional interim pastor is a change agent charged with the specific, temporary task of guiding a church through a season of healing, reconciliation, and systemic change.

Beyond this, we have served hundreds of pastors and lay leaders in conflict reconciliation and spiritual formation. Hardly a week goes by that we do not receive a call from a pastor, denomination leader, or elder seeking advice and counsel for an urgent conflict.

The following pages will reveal stories of real people and actual churches in conflict (though all names have been changed).[1] You will undoubtedly see yourself and your situation in some of these accounts. More important, you will be guided to look into Scripture for principles and procedures you can use in your church to anticipate and resolve conflict and, in many cases, prevent it altogether.

While we will recommend many practical principles you may apply to your church, *Making Peace* is a "why" book, not a "how-to" book. The lordship of Jesus Christ, not method, should be the object and subject of your search for answers. If you are in conflict now, I commend you first to prayer and to the Scriptures before applying any principle in this book. Ask the Holy Spirit to guide you into truth and to give you discernment. Ultimately this book is not about conflict as much as it is about the church, about what we have lost and what God desires His people to become.

Do not use this book as a proof text to bolster your argument for any given dispute. As George MacDonald once wrote, "Few men do more harm than those who, taking the right side, dispute for personal victory, and argue, as they are then sure to do, ungenerously."[2]

God would rather you be reconciled than right. A broken and contrite heart is what God desires.

Making Peace is divided into three parts. Part 1 is essential to understanding the theological and ecclesiological foundations for resolving church conflict. Read this first. If you are desperate for answers addressed in later chapters, I still urge you to read chapters 1 through 3 first. A primary premise of this book is that reconciliation is not a set of principles to be followed but a life to be lived. In fact, the principles and methods offered in this book are powerless apart from your receiving the fundamental call to embody a way of life shaped by the Cross.

We'll explore the root causes of conflict and theological basis for the church as the instrument of reconciliation in chapters 1 and 2. In chapter 3 we'll see what spiritual leadership would look like in a church that embodies biblical community.

Part 2 introduces the premise that all church conflict is always about leadership. How leaders respond to conflict determines if, when, and how the conflict is reconciled. Chapter 4 explores a biblical view of conflict with a challenge to see every conflict as an opportunity to claim and take part in God's redemptive purpose. We are, all of us, called to a ministry of reconciliation; that is, living into the grace we claim.

Chapters 5 through 8 discuss the four common response styles to conflict. You will find yourself in one or more of these styles. Each is negative and will always make the conflict worse. Yet we employ these passive, evasive, defensive, or aggressive conflict styles because they are habits and practices that have been learned and hardened over a life of disagreements and struggles. They have become part of our character, a way of thinking and acting that God wants to transform. By identifying your conflict response style, windows for redemptive change will be opened. Chapter 9 discusses "triangulation" and the difference between authentic and counterfeit peace.

Part 3 moves from what we are doing wrong to how to do things right. Chapter 10 defines submission and why it is essential for the church to be the church. Chapter 11 describes how authentic communication opens the way for reconciliation through one of the most important biblical principles for embodying peace—speaking the truth in love. Chapter 12 is about confession and forgiveness— why each is necessary if we are to build authentic, redemptive communities. Chapter 13 discusses how discipline and restitution are necessary to restore the sinner. The book concludes with a call to repentance in seven key areas of the church.

The promise of Scripture is that God will allow nothing into your life that you are not able to bear through faith in Him. Whatever conflict or crisis you may now be facing, God will provide a way out or a way through for your good and His glory.

Notes

1. All the stories and examples cited in this book are true, though I have intentionally changed or distorted some of the stories to ensure confidentiality while trying to retain the integrity of the original circumstances. In most cases, the events and sins described are now reconciled under the blood of Jesus Christ and, therefore, no longer exist. Here, as in all things, focus should not be given to individuals or events but to the lordship of Jesus Christ.
2. George MacDonald, *Paul Faber, Surgeon* (Whitethorn, Calif.: Johannesen, 1992), 156. Originally published by Hurst & Blackett (London) in 1879.

PROLOGUE:
CONFLICTS AT SECOND CHURCH ... AND ELSEWHERE

W hen Tim announced his resignation as senior pastor at Second Church, the congregation was bewildered, hurt, and divided. Tim's vague reference to "personal issues" and "past failures" in his statement to the congregation only added to the confusion.

Second Church was a lighthouse evangelical church in the region. The church had seen significant growth in attendance and conversions over Tim's ten-year pastorate. Tim was a very personable and popular young leader and enthusiastic preacher. He was well loved.

Still, there were signs that something at Second Church was amiss. During the previous year, one associate pastor and two elders had resigned with little or no explanation. Attendance seemed to be dipping. Giving was down. Grumbling was on the rise.

These are common symptoms for troubled or conflicted churches. Often, awareness of a problem starts with a vague feeling that something is not quite right. Then something happens—a sin, disappointment, or failure—that seems to explain the problem. Usually, however, the event is a symptom of a deeper problem. Reconciliation requires courage to discover and lovingly address the underlying problem.

All conflict hurts. Hurt can be good or bad. Reconciliation depends upon how we respond to the conflict and deal with the hurt. The story of Second Church will illustrate how bad conflict can be, and how far hurt can go, when we fail to uncover and address root causes of our conflicts. (We point out that Tim and Nancy's story is extreme. The symptoms and circumstances of your conflict may be quite different, but the principles for reconciliation are the same.)

Rumors about trouble in Tim and Nancy's marriage had been rippling through the congregation for months—ever since Tim and Nancy took a three-month sabbatical together. Tim had told the deacon board privately that he and Nancy were struggling. Tim did not explain what the problem was, saying only that it was "personal." The board did not inquire further. Instead, the board encouraged Tim and Nancy to go away for marriage counseling. The deacons announced the sabbatical to the church and asked for prayer.

When Tim and Nancy returned, Tim thanked the church for helping save his marriage. He said he learned that his "workaholic hours" had led him to neglect and hurt his family. He was determined to change. People assumed that the problem was over.

Not long after this, though, people started noticing that Nancy and the kids were increasingly distant from Tim, often alone in the parsonage. Few in the congregation had any idea what was wrong, so members were shocked when they heard Nancy was filing for divorce.

The news split the church between loyalties and accusations for and against Tim and Nancy. Some believed Tim was at fault, others blamed Nancy. Members blamed leaders. A few claimed it was all the "attack of Satan to destroy our church."

In the months following Tim's resignation, weekly attendance at Second Church dropped from an average of 535 to about 425 people. Many who left Second Church were leaders, and those who kept coming stopped giving. By the time the deacons called us in to help assess and repair the damage, the church was in chaos.

When our team arrived at the church, Tim and Nancy's divorce was final—hurried through the courts in a matter of months. During our lunch together, Tim explained that repeated confessions to counselors and many attempts at restoring his marriage had failed. "I have poured my life out," Tim told me, "and it has cost me everything." Tim was worried that our assessment would affect his future plans. He told me that he wanted to "move on" with his life.

Nancy was still living in the church parsonage. There were rumors she was battling suicide and depression. Many were concerned for her health.

The congregation was about to discover much more. As we interviewed people throughout the assessment weekend, the following sequence of events emerged.

Before coming to Second Church ten years earlier, Tim was youth pastor in a church of the same denomination. Tim devoted himself to ministry, spending all his time with teens, particularly one teenage girl. The relationship with this girl eventually led to sex.

Tim felt tremendous guilt about his sin. He met with the girl's parents to apologize. Outraged, the parents threatened to sue Tim and the church. A district leader of the denomination was called in to meet with the family. They agreed not to press charges or tell the church about the sin if Tim agreed to resign and leave the church immediately. Tim agreed.

The district leader felt compassion for Tim, who was shaken and remorseful. The district leader felt that Tim had learned from his "mistake" and, since he apologized already, saying or doing more would "just make the matter worse." In fact, the district leader offered to find Tim another church. So Tim resigned immediately, saying that he "wanted to pursue ministry opportunities elsewhere." No mention was ever made of the sin.

A few months later, Tim applied to be pastor at Second Church. The district leader gave a strong recommendation. No one on the search committee asked Tim why he left his former church. Neither the district leader nor Tim made any mention of the past. The people of Second Church liked and embraced Tim immediately and called him to be their senior pastor.

Tim told me that he never lied to the search committee or the congregation. In fact, he said that he had always wanted to say something to the church but the district leader advised him against it. So Tim told no one. He plunged into ministry at Second Church determined to put his past behind him. The church grew. People were saved. Still, Tim never felt right about keeping the secret. So one day, after many years at Second Church, Tim shared his secret with one of the associate pastors. Tim told him all about the sin and why he left the former church. Tim felt relieved to have the truth out. He told no one else.

Months later, when Tim borrowed his associate's computer, he discovered pornographic Web sites that the associate pastor had bookmarked on his Internet browser for downloading and viewing in his office. Tim was shocked and angry. He called the associate pastor into his office to confront him, demanding that he confess his sin to the deacons. If the associate pastor did not go to the deacons, Tim said, "I was going to tell them myself."

The associate pastor responded with a threat of his own. "If you tell the deacons about me," he said, "I'll tell the deacons about you."

Stalemate. Both pastors had a damaging secret about the other. So they agreed not to tell either story. Instead, Tim arranged for the associate pastor to resign and find another church "to pursue other ministry opportunities."

As our weekend at Second Church unfolded, more secrets were exposed. We learned that three more leaders in the church had committed adultery with women in the congregation during the past several years. No sin was ever specifically acknowledged or publicly confessed. Leaders just suddenly resigned or left the church under a cloud of mystery. Spouses from two of the broken marriages still attended worship services, sitting on opposite sides of the sanctuary, each refusing to talk with the other.

In all, we documented numerous cases of sexual immorality at Second Church, including adultery, lust, pornography, pedophilia, and homosexuality. The sins involved former members *and* leaders reaching back at least a dozen years through, and up to, the time of our assessment. Other sins, such as gossip and dissension among leadership and membership, were also widespread. Our task was to tell the church.

This story, with a script fit for a seedy soap opera, is true. It actually occurred in a leading evangelical church that we served. The sin at Second Church was alarming. But this sin is not about sexual sin or any other of the sins that plague our churches—from gossip to grandstanding. The conflict at Second Church, and every other conflict, including the one you may be facing right now, is not, in the end, about sin. Conflict reveals our faith and character: our willingness or refusal to be the body of Christ. As much as Tim and others were responsible for their sin, the church also failed to recognize and address sin in the early stages. The church failed to be the church.

When we peel back the pages of this horrible story we begin to see dozens of opportunities missed that could have prevented, or at least addressed, the sin in the first place. Second Church's situation reveals the common mistakes and oversights that can lead a church into deeper trouble. They include:

1. *Lack of community.* How many people saw a problem in Tim's character when he was growing up, attending seminary, or serving as a young pastor, but said nothing about it? Where were the senior pastor, deacons, and godly friends to encourage, warn, and correct Tim before his behavior led to sin? The church must be a place where we invite fellow believers to speak truth and love into our lives.

2. *Worldly privacy.* How many times did friends, fellow leaders, and Christian brothers and sisters choose to look the other way or not interfere because Tim's behavior happened outside the church building and his "private" life was "none of their business"?

3. *Shifting responsibility.* Did you notice how many times leaders ignored or shifted responsibility for loving discipline and restoration? The denominational leader allowed Tim to leave without

confession, restitution, or restoration. He was never asked to submit to a process to reconstitute his character. At Second Church, when leaders realized Tim and Nancy were struggling, the immediate remedy was to send the couple outside the fellowship for "help." What is the church for, if not this?

4. *Avoidance.* No one on the search committee asked Tim why he left his former church. No one at his present church asked him what the real problem was in his life and marriage. Instead, both Tim and the church were constantly trying to "fix" the problem by assuming the best and hoping the problem went away. They ignored warning signs, kept silent, or named the sin something else.

5. *Fear of lawsuits.* The fear or threat of legal action caused Tim's first church to encourage Tim to leave quickly; the threat caused Tim to accept the blackmail of his associate pastor. It's as if each person said, "We can't obey Scripture or trust the power of God because, if we did, we might get sued."

6. *Cheap grace.* Tim and Second Church told themselves it's grace to keep the sin secret. Actually, it's deception. Many church leaders today follow the same distorted logic. Remorse or sorrow does not equal restoration. Keeping sin in the dark sustains sin's power, because it keeps the sinner from genuine fellowship and robs the person of the forgiveness and restoration made possible through the Cross. It is never loving or gracious to cover over sin, or to merely forgive and forget.

Resolving conflict requires a way of obeying that confronts our popular notions of privacy with a truth and grace that recognizes the power of the Cross. To make peace the church must embody the principles and practices of reconciliation made possible through the life, death, and resurrection of Jesus Christ. Reconciliation is a way of life. To do this, the church must recover biblical community. The church that is redemptive will learn to practice reconciliation as a way of life.

Part 1

THE MESS
WE ARE IN

Church conflict is neither isolated nor uncommon. Indeed, church pastors, governing boards, and denominational leaders spend a major portion of their time each year assessing, mediating, and reconciling church conflicts. They are called upon to:

- Discipline or remove lay leadership for sin or division
- Discipline disruptive and divisive church members
- Mediate manipulation and control issues rising from "gatekeepers and power brokers"
- Resolve conflict between boards, staff, and members—on issues from facilities to worship style
- Confront gossip, consumerism, individualism, and a critical spirit among members
- Negotiate competing leader/member assumptions and expectations about future vision
- Confront members and leaders who are resisting change
- Discipline or remove pastor(s) for sin; that is, sexual immorality, lying, etc.

How is it that so many churches are in trouble, conflict, or decline? What is it about us—who we are, what we think, and how we act—that conflict is so prevalent?

In the next few chapters we will explore the foundations of church conflict. Two summary points can be made here to frame our thinking.

First, church conflict is always theological, never merely interpersonal. There are many causes and reasons for church conflict, including cultural, spiritual, and structural factors. But all church conflict has theological roots. For instance, the common dispute between contemporary and traditional worship style is fundamentally a theological issue. If you doubt this, listen to the arguments posed for and against each side, then ask, "Who is the subject and object of debate?" You will find that we are talking about ourselves, not God. We miss what and Who worship is for.

The church is a living organism, not a machine; a body, not a collection of individuals. In the church, all interpersonal disputes are symptoms of deeper problems impacting or involving the whole body. This is what makes church conflict different from all others, because the church is founded upon oneness in Christ: "There is one body and one Spirit—just as you were called to one hope when you were called—one Lord, one faith, one baptism; one God and Father of all, who is over all and through all and in all" (Ephesians 4: 4–6). Nothing touches one member of the body that does not touch us all. Efforts to restore and reconcile personal relationships without addressing the underlying systemic and theological roots will always be inadequate.

Second, all church conflict is always about leadership, character, and community. Conflict reveals who we really are. Leadership is not the cause of all conflict. In our experience, conflict comes more from the pews than the pulpit. However, the way leadership responds to the conflict will always determine if, how, and when the conflict is reconciled. The problem is that most church leaders have little or no practical training in biblical conflict resolution.

Regardless of skill or training, a leader will respond to conflict out of his or her character far more than knowledge. Conflict reveals the true character of a leader. Jesus told His disciples, "You have heard that it was said, 'Love your neighbor and hate your enemy.' But I tell you: Love your enemies and pray for those who persecute you, that you may be sons of your Father in heaven. . . . If you love those who love you, what reward will you get? Are not even the tax collectors doing that?" (Matthew 5:43–46). Who we are is revealed by how we react to persecution.

Character, like righteousness, is formed, not possessed. Spiritual character is God's work in us through His Word, by His Spirit, and in His community. Unfortunately, many of us are formed more by secular than spiritual forces. In either case, we become who we are together. If we gather, as the world does, around values of individualism, then we form self-absorbed people whose empty lives demand a constant fight (or flight) for individual rights and needs. But if we gather in authentic community hungering and thirsting for righteousness, we have God's blessing and filling to grow through our differences (Matthew 5:6). Community is revealed by how we meet at the Communion table.

To understand these points more clearly, we need to explore the foundations of conflict and community.

ROOT CAUSES
OF CONFLICT

*For he chose us in him before the creation of the world
to be holy and blameless in his sight.*

~ EPHESIANS 1:4

The words were printed in large letters on bright fluorescent colored signs: "Frost Heaves." They looked like placards from a low-budget political campaign stuck in the snow. Some guys named Frost and Heaves were running for national office.

People who live in northern New England know that *frost heaves* are not the names of politicians or a type of ice cream. The two words describe what happens to our roads in March and April. They freeze and heave.

Frost heaves are caused during winter by thawing daytime temperatures followed by freezing nighttime temperatures. When water that has collected in pockets underneath the road surface freezes, the expanding ice forces the road upward, often cracking open the surface an inch or two at the peak.

Frost heaves can cause roads to rise as much as six inches, and they usually damage road surfaces permanently. Driving a vehicle too fast over a frost heave can damage your shocks and shock your nerves.

One nine-mile stretch of road between our home and the next town must be one of the world's worst roads for frost heaves. In some sections of the road, drivers who hit the heave just right can serve dinner, view an in-flight movie, and earn five hundred frequent flier miles before landing on the other side. Well, so it seems.

When the weather breaks to temperatures consistently above freezing, the road settles down to its previous level with potholes and cracks. Eventually the road crew dutifully fills in the gaps, solving the problem until the next winter.

People complain a lot about the roads and those who crew them. But the real problem is underneath. And that's the way it is in most churches. The real conflict lies below the surface.

What is presented as the "problem" is usually a symptom of what lies underneath. As long as we treat the symptom, not the underlying problem, the conflict will return. It may lie dormant for a time, but it always comes back. Always.

In our work with dozens of conflicted churches, four systemic issues have emerged that, like water trapped under heaving roads, are the source of most crises. They are cultural, structural, spiritual, and theological issues that we must not ignore.

CULTURAL ISSUES

Many Western churches look and act more like the contemporary culture than the kingdom of Christ. The term for such behavior is *cultural syncretism.*

By *culture* we mean a complex system of assumptions, practices, stories, and beliefs that guide how a common people think and act as well as what they value. For instance, "meeting my personal needs" is an everyday assumption and behavior in a consumer culture. Christianity is formed around a different story—Jesus' death on the cross—requiring a different set of assumptions and practices that considers the needs of others before our own. (See Philippians 2:3–8.)

Syncretism is the uncritical combination of two or more different, often opposing, beliefs and practices into one. For instance, Western culture celebrates individualism and self-promotion. Christianity calls believers to love and serve others. These stories and values are fundamentally opposed. Western individualism actively persuades against spiritual vitality and mutuality, breeding autonomy instead of biblical community.

By attempting to harmonize secular values with historic Christian ideals, we unwittingly adopt habits, therapies, and practices that undermine our call to be a separate and holy people.

In our churches, this has both practical and theological implications. When believers look like the world, they lose their distinctive voices. They do not "shine like stars" in darkness but join in the parade. We must watch ourselves closely to see if salvation and sanctification, God's great gifts to the church, have become privatized and co-opted into a personal transaction.

Are we gathering in community to practice and prove a way of life together, or are we privatizing faith into self-help answers that breed a kind of spiritual attention deficit disorder? Where is reverent waiting, corporate intercession, and public confession in the contemporary church?

CHURCHES FOCUSED ON INDIVIDUAL NEEDS

These cultural conditions impact our ability to address conflict redemptively. A church founded on principles of individualism will respond to conflict out of its cultural values. Since conflict threatens private faith, we respond with the democratic ideals that form our privacy. Issues of fairness and tolerance take precedence over obedience and mutual submission.

In many churches, the remedy for conflict often makes it worse, deepening the problem by failing to address the fundamental issue: We are trusting our ways more than God's.

All individualism leads to consumerism. When self is center, the world exists to meet one's personal needs. "Hey, I'm entitled to this!" A culture of consumerism will always value individual needs above community life. "You're important to me so long as you serve my needs."

When a church focuses on meeting the needs of individuals, Jesus and the Bible become a personal, need-meeting machine. The church becomes a collection of individuals who are fundamentally at competition with one another—competing to have their needs met. Here, the Gospel becomes a commodity distributed by supply and demand. Since no church can meet all the needs, ultimately one set of needs must be placed against the other.

When this happens, staff and members will compete to make a case for how and why their needs are greater than others. To make more compelling cases, the church becomes divided into interest groups or coalitions formed by age and individual preference.

To address these concerns, some churches offer solutions that only compound the problem. The answer, they believe, is targeting ministries and services to specific demographic or life interest groups who have the same concerns, desires, or needs. This keeps people happy for a time but further fragments the body. The attempt to meet selfish needs tends to reinforce selfishness.

The worship wars are a good example. In many churches the style of worship pits believer against believer. Coalitions form to lobby a point of view. Members are too busy counting how many hymns and how many choruses are sung in each service to actually worship God.

Instead of asking, "How can we enter into worship in mutual submission under the lordship of Jesus Christ?" we divide ourselves, forming two or three worship services according to music style. In effect we become multiple, homogeneous interest groups sharing, or fighting over, the same space. We are not the church.

Our fighting resembles our values as well. To defend our point of view, we quote Scriptures that prove how we are right and the other is wrong. We divide over narrow and legalistic notions of truth. One small church we served actually had two youth groups—one for home-school kids and the other for Christian school and public school children.

Or we separate people by having special services and support groups for the divorced, for singles and single moms, or for people with addictive behaviors. Most churches think nothing of sending their members outside the church for private therapy conducted by "experts" who are not accountable to the church and often not believers.

Well-intentioned efforts to help the hurting often miss, or deny, the power of healing given to the church. These approaches are forming us—and the church—in ways we do not see.

The church becomes a shopping center where we pick and choose what is good for us. We are not a community being formed by God's Word and Spirit. We are individuals shaping ourselves. This strips the Gospel of its power—leaving people in their selfish individualism rather than inviting them into a transforming community of faith.

CHRISTIANITY AND SELF-HELP

Christianity is not a "self-help" religion. Salvation is not a private decision, nor is sanctification a personal transaction. These are Western values. This is individualism, not discipleship; a cheap substitute for biblical faith.

A church that organizes itself around meeting personal needs runs the great, unintended risk of breeding autonomy rather than mutuality. It also risks a theology of prosperity (feel good now) rather than a theology of the Cross (suffering for the joy set before us). God wants us to be healthy in ways greater than our perceived needs and feelings.

We must ask ourselves hard questions about the faith people are being saved into, when our spirituality becomes self-conscious instead of Christ-revealing.

The trends above are occurring in both traditional and contemporary churches. Each trains people to think and to act more like individuals and less like a body. Transactional churches form consumers, not parishioners. These are the seeds of conflict.

How Do We Measure Fruit?

Years ago I wrote for a marketing firm that served many large, national Christian organizations. To encourage greater giving, the marketing firm I worked for frequently included an offer in its fundraising appeal. "If you send a gift of $25 today, we'll send you a copy of [Famous Pastor's] most recent book."

It worked. More people gave in order to get something back. Our marketing firm argued, as marketing executives do, that we were being successful because the donor list was growing and more people were giving. This was half true. It was an argument from quantity, not quality. For instance, no one asked what kind of donors we were forming.

For our Christian clients we could spiritualize our success by saying our efforts were "bearing fruit." No one thought to ask, "What kind of fruit?" This question leads us to the problem with every marketing-driven strategy. What, or who, are we forming? Are we forming believers or consumers?

Our fund raising, in the end, actually had little to do with philanthropy. We were not attracting donors; we were building a book club. There is a qualitative difference between someone who gives in order to get something back and someone who gives for the joy of giving. Giving to the poor for a tax deduction is not the same as giving to feed and clothe the poor.

This same dynamic applies to the church. It is not enough to measure fruit by building facilities, increasing programs, and growing attendance. We must ask, "What kind of fruit are we forming?"

WHAT KIND OF PEOPLE ARE WE FORMING?

Think for a moment about why people go to your church.

Of the more than 5,000 people we have interviewed during the past eight years, in traditional as well as contemporary churches, most believers evaluate their church positively or negatively in consumer, transactional terms. Christians choose a church for the same inclinations and motivations that they choose a supermarket.

Q. Why do you go to Grace Church?
A. Because I like the music.
Q. Why do you go to Shaw's Supermarket?
A. Because I like the produce section.

Christians have come to view the church with the same habits of thinking and patterns of practice as every other aspect of our consumer culture. We shop for church the way we shop for melons.

Some argue that this is inevitable and expected in our culture. If we are to reach our world we need to speak its language. The church must be relevant if it is to be serious and focused on reaching the lost.

The fact is, all churches employ some kind of marketing, whether it is a sign out front or announcements in the bulletin. Marketing is not evil, but it is not theologically or spiritually neutral either.

There is no question that marketing works in a consumer culture. Many unbelievers have found Christ, and many "nominal Christians" have found their way back to the church. We ought to have the apostle Paul's passion for reaching the lost.

Though I am free and belong to no man, I make myself a slave to everyone, to win as many as possible. To the Jews I became like a Jew, to win the Jews. To those under the law I became like one under the law (though I myself am not under the law), so as to win those under the law. To those not having the law I became like one not having the law (though I am not free from God's law but am under Christ's law), so as to win those not having the law. To the weak I became weak, to win the weak. I have become all things to all men so that by all possible means I might save some. I do all this for the sake of the gospel, that I may share in its blessings. (1 Corinthians 9:19–23)

The question is whether the methods that are so useful in attracting people to faith are in any way sufficient to grow believers to maturity.

The problem with infant Christians is they are, well, infantile. Like babies, they tend to whine or cry when something they want is changed or taken away. The writers of two New Testament letters cautioned immature, nongrowing Christians:

I gave you milk, not solid food, for you were not yet ready for it. Indeed, you are still not ready. (1 Corinthians 3:2)

In fact, though by this time you ought to be teachers, you need someone to teach you the elementary truths of God's word all over again. You need milk, not solid food! Anyone who lives on milk, being still an infant, is not acquainted with the teaching about righteousness. (Hebrews 5:12–13)

Young believers can quickly revert to the values of contemporary culture—insisting on their way by having a vote and lobbying for their point of view. This leads to coalitions, politics, and efforts to control. Lost is a community of righteousness where God's will is worked out through mutual submission, speaking the truth in love, repentance, and forgiveness.

"THE CUSTOMER IS ALWAYS RIGHT"

Means shape ends. Certain methods bear certain kinds of fruit. When the church becomes a place of transactions we make to get what we need or want, God becomes a product made after our consumer tastes and desires. We would never say this, of course, but these habits and practices are woven into the fabric of market-driven approaches. In reality, the credo is "The customer is always right."

Where you start has direct impact on where you end up. If the starting point is self, it is very difficult to end with the lordship of Jesus Christ. Church leadership structures also illustrate this principle. Autocratic structures appeal to people who need and want order in their lives. God is the lawgiver. Democratic structures attract people who want to feel better about their lives and themselves. God becomes the need-meeter. In each, Christianity becomes something we control and do alone. We make God in our image, not ourselves in His.

Contrast this to the Bible's description of the church as a people who gather for and with others at the foot of the cross:

> Do nothing out of selfish ambition or vain conceit, but in humility consider others better than yourselves. Each of you should look not only to your own interests, but also to the interests of others. Your attitude should be the same as that of Christ Jesus: Who, being in very nature God, did not consider equality with God something to be grasped, but made himself nothing, taking the very nature of a servant, being made in human likeness. And being found in appearance as a man, he humbled himself and became obedient to death—even death on a cross! (Philippians 2:3–8)

A church organized around meeting needs breeds selfishness, and it inevitably leads to competition, control, and conflict. The apostle James says as much:

> What causes fights and quarrels among you? Don't they come from your desires that battle within you? You want something but don't get it. You kill and covet, but you cannot have what you want. You quarrel and fight. You do not have, because you do not ask God. When

you ask, you do not receive, because you ask with wrong motives, that you may spend what you get on your pleasures. You adulterous people, don't you know that friendship with the world is hatred toward God? Anyone who chooses to be a friend of the world becomes an enemy of God. (James 4:1–5)

WHERE GOD FORMS HIS PEOPLE

Is your church actually encouraging people to think and act like the world? Are you forming believers who are not a "people"?

The church is the spiritual "place" where God forms His people. We are chosen to be people who are being transformed into Christlikeness. The problem is that we have become so accustomed to thinking and acting like individuals we cannot even see or accept that we are forming selfishness, not godliness—until a conflict or crisis arises. God has called us into a kingdom much greater than our selfish needs, dull familiarity, and easy assumptions.

Scripture stands in stark contrast to the narcissistic and autonomous thinking of our self-absorbed world. God wants to remake and redeem our needs before He meets them. He calls us into a culture formed by the Cross.

STRUCTURAL ISSUES

All conflict is complex. The natural human response to conflict is to simplify and, at times, to vilify. The complex evidence surrounding the conflict is often ambiguous and contradictory, and individuals and coalitions trying to make sense of it will describe competing views of reality based upon partial facts or events. These descriptions may be compelling in part, but ultimately inadequate to explain the whole.

Often people on all sides of a conflict will tend to minimize their personal responsibility while seeking to blame or disparage others. In extreme situations, some will seek to elevate themselves or try to strengthen their position by demonizing or negating others.

SEEING THE SYSTEM DYNAMIC

These inadequate conflict responses are part of the "system dynamic"[1] that creates the climate for the conflict as well as increases the time and effort it will take to resolve it. By *system dynamic* we mean the interrelationship of external and internal forces that influence our decisions and create the conditions for conflict. A system dynamic is a structure that underlies the way we organize, work, lead, and make decisions in organizations, including churches.

For instance, members of Third Church were in deep conflict concerning why the elders had "forced" a pastor to resign. Wanting to simplify, some said the issue was racism. Others said it was about flaws and failure in the pastor's character. Still others mentioned financial pressures. All of these forces and more were part of the system that created the conflict in the first place and influenced negative responses to the conflict that made the crisis worse.

In our final report to Third Church, we wrote the following to explain our call for systemic change by asking all leaders to resign:

> *Our assessment found multiple patterns of thinking and habits of acting by individuals and the church that are part of the culture of the church. That is, the findings reveal systemic as well as personal failure. These represent fundamental spiritual and theological issues that must be examined, explored, and addressed. Habits formed and practiced over many years do not change easily or quickly. They do not go away merely by saying, "I'm sorry," or, "You are forgiven."*

Rather, transformation will require dedicated time and submission to a process that will:

~ examine, identify, and confess past failure;

- ∾ identify root needs, causes, or flaws in character, behavior, or thinking;

- ∾ unlearn negative habits practiced over time;

- ∾ relearn new habits of behavior and thinking; and

- ∾ reconstitute personal character and church culture.

To change any system, one must change the underlying structure—the system dynamic. Any change that fails to address the underlying structure is insufficient.

By suspending and temporarily replacing the role and function of present leadership, all church members and leaders will learn new ways to think and act together while depending upon God's Spirit rather than human effort.

This is a thoroughly biblical principle. Throughout the Old and New Testaments, and especially in the ministry of Jesus, God brings spiritual transformation by turning the assumptions and expectations of His people upside-down, *often by placing His people in a position where they must trust God completely.* Spiritual transformation often follows systemic change.

As long as the church focused on one part of the system, not the whole, complete reconciliation was not possible. Reconciling a systemic conflict must be adequate to address or account for all the underlying forces in the system.

Of course, this means to be redemptive we have to think and discern systemically. But this is what is missing in most leadership and reconciliation models for the church. That is, we train leaders to lead and to reconcile in ways that follow the cultural and structural assumptions that create the climate for conflict in the first place.

Many seminaries recruit and train pastors to think, speak, and act alone. Few seminaries teach pastors how to build and work with an interdependent team, or how to anticipate and reconcile patterns of sin and corporate conflict. Though church conflict is widespread in the West, most church leaders have no formal or practical training in confronting and resolving conflict. Further, most resources published to assist leaders through church conflict teach that all conflict is interpersonal. Conflict is interpersonal and a lot more.

Too often pastors address problems from within the flawed assumptions of their culture and training. Unable to see how problems are forming, and how their leadership is often a cause, church leaders employ legalistic or democratic remedies to issues that require Spirit-directed discernment, repentance, and forgiveness. Meanwhile, leaders have to deal with members who, as noted above, insist on rights and want to "vote" instead of submit.

Treating the Dynamic in Right- and Left-Handed Ways

So leaders resort to right-handed and left-handed ways of leading in order to gain control or keep the peace.

Right-handed leaders will try to keep order by centralizing power. A right-handed pastor will preach about submission and authority while employing a hierarchical, top-down management style that often becomes legalistic. The result is a church organized to protect a leader instead of to point to Christ.

Left-handed leaders think and act in the opposite direction, encouraging a decentralized, unfocused form of management that fails to lead or to grow a people. Here the object and subject is also the leader, who will often elicit sympathy by playing the wounded victim. The result is a Christian landscape that compromises truth to keep the peace. (More on the right-handed and left-handed philosophies and practices will come in chapter 2.)

We find leaders like this because we unintentionally form them. Few seminaries screen their graduates for character or calling. Instead they continue to produce leaders who are guided by knowledge and methods centered on a structure that fits their training or gifting.

If the leader is a teacher, the church is built around the pulpit ministry. Monologue is the primary means of communication—people sitting passively listening to the pastor expound. If the pastor is an evangelist, the church will be built on attracting and saving unbelievers.

In these and many other cases, the leader often works alone instead of building an interdependent team. Often a pastor will resist building a team because he is easily threatened by others who may be gifted in areas he is not. When these pastors do assemble a team, it is often made up of people who pose no threat to the pastor because they either think alike or are less gifted than the pastor.

So our churches grow and suffer in direct proportion to the strengths and weaknesses of one person. These leaders model autonomy, not community. The church easily falls into conflicts and cults of personality.

Church constitutions and bylaws reveal the same weaknesses. Wooden and institutional, these documents often lack a spiritual vitality, deferring instead to objective rules or subjective ideals that fail to address underlying structures and ignore or undercut biblical principles. Many remedies presume a spiritual maturity seldom present.

To address these issues systemically we have to ask what forces are guiding us. All of these are structural, systemic problems that foster conflict.

Spiritual Issues

As we have just seen, much of church conflict can be understood by its cultural and structural origins. These external forces contribute to but are secondary to a more fundamental root cause of church conflict—a spiritual one.

When a Knowing or Feeling Faith Replaces a Living Faith

Many of our churches have lost (or never found) a balanced understanding of holiness and application of the person and work of the Holy Spirit. We do not know what it means or what it would look like to live in, walk by, and sow to the Holy Spirit. All that is left is a notion—not a real living—of holiness, a preoccupation with a right-handed knowing or a left-handed feeling faith.

For some churches, knowing Scripture is everything. If we were to draw a figure representing this "knowing" faith, we would draw a huge head atop a stick-figure frame. In other churches, experiencing God or reaching the lost is so consuming that, to picture them, we would draw obese frames supporting a tiny head or brain. Feeling churches can often become like the Corinthians, "a mile wide but an inch thick," while rational churches can become like Pharisees, arrogant and self-righteous.

When all the data is in, we are most in conflict because we are not what we claim to be. Our churches lack "spiritual authenticity." We claim to be crucified with Christ, but it is "I" who lives, not Christ. We think and act with our personal needs first in mind. We claim to be forgiven, but we refuse to confess or forgive, excusing ourselves and blaming others. We claim to honor and submit to leaders while we gossip about them and attack their authority. We claim to be the bride of Christ while divorce and marital infidelity thrive in both pulpit and pew.

Who are we trying to fool, God or ourselves?

Many of our churches are sick and dying because they are pretending to be the church. Worse, many of us are invested in our dysfunction. We do not really want to be well; we just want to feel better. We want the problem to go away. But we do not want to pay the price. Our identity has been formed around our pathologies.

The pagan world looks on and sees no viable contrast, no difference affected by the life, death, and resurrection of Jesus Christ. The Cross is robbed of its power.

BEING HOLY—TOGETHER

The Gospel offers the power to change our lives, to renounce our past, and to form new habits of righteousness. God instituted the church as the social, spiritual realm for this transformation to take place. When the church gathers in mutual love and submission under God's Word and Spirit, we have the opportunity to hear God speak in ways that change and form us. This is our calling: to be separate and holy. "But just as he who called you is holy, so be holy in all you do; for it is written: 'Be holy, because I am holy'" (1 Peter 1:15–16).

This is not news, of course, but it is rarely practiced. When preached it is usually objectified into some legalistic rules or impersonal exhortation to change. "God says, 'to be holy, do this . . .'"

We have lost the sense of what it means to be a holy people. We are not a called-out, called-together, spiritual house where God is forming us. Consequently, we are not forming people around the character of God. We may fill heads with great knowledge and fill hearts with good feeling, but we frequently forget the tangible ways God has given us to reconstitute our lives in Christlikeness.

Reconciling conflict is not about knowing or feeling. It is about obeying and being. That is, holiness is a craft, a discipline that requires a community of others to practice. We cannot be holy alone.

Further, God says, "Be holy," not, "Do holy," or, "Think holy." Thinking and doing follow sacrifice and transformation (1 John 3:18). Christians are called to be transformed: "Do not conform any longer to the pattern of this world, but be transformed by the renewing of your mind. Then you will be able to test and approve what God's will is—his good, pleasing and perfect will" (Romans 12:2).

The test of transformation does not end with the renewed mind. The renewed mind must result in specific habits and practices that test and prove God's will. God appoints the church to be the place where this happens.

Not long ago I had a conversation with a Christian leader about Christian virtues and character. I suggested that virtues are formed in the church. My friend protested this and argued that many virtues, such as honesty, could be learned outside of the church, even alone.

"Yes," I replied, "but honesty outside the church is not Christian honesty."

A person need not be a Christian to be honest. But Christian honesty or truth-telling is different in form and purpose. It is formed by the description and discovery of what it means to follow Jesus Christ, who is Truth. Truth cleans and grows the church up into Christ.[2]

It is in the body of Christ that our virtues find authentic meaning and life. There is no Christianity in Scripture outside of the church. There are no Lone Ranger Christians.

Most Christians know what is right and wrong. They know God desires holiness. But many Christians have no idea how holiness might happen in the context of others. They come to church but remain alone to follow their feelings, rules, or methods. When they fail, they must hide their sins for fear they might be found out or run out of the church.

The point of the Cross, of the church, and of Scripture is that you cannot change yourself. Change is the work of God operating through His Word, His Spirit, and His people. All three are necessary.

THEOLOGICAL ISSUES

Finally, there is a theological root to our conflicts. By theology we mean the study of God—who He is and what He requires of His people. In this sense we combine theology with ecclesiology—the study of the church.

All church conflict is theological. Our theology has more often been shaped by—rather than transform—the cultural, structural, and spiritual aberrations discussed above.

INTEGRITY VERSUS AUTONOMY

One example of this is the way our understanding of church unity has changed from spiritual integrity to spiritual autonomy.

The English word for *integrity* comes from the word *integer*, referring to a "whole number," a "complete entity," or something "undivided." In the church, integrity means being undivided in your relationship to God, yourself, and others. Integrity requires community, a collective commitment to "one Lord, one faith, one baptism; one God and Father of all, who is over all and through all and in all." While many speak of "integrity" and "community," most Western churches are spiritually and functionally autonomous.

The word *autonomy* comes from the Greek *autonomia,* meaning "self-ruling." To be autonomous means to be independent and self-governing. In the church, this has come to mean individual privacy, preferences, and rights on personal and corporate levels. It accounts for the rise of independent and nondenomination churches as well as democratic governing structures.

Integrity and autonomy offer two radically different kinds of "oneness." Autonomy celebrates independence and self—one alone. Integrity celebrates interdependence—two or more becoming one together. The Western church has replaced integrity with autonomy.

SPIRITUAL INTEGRITY: A COMMON BIBLICAL THEME

Spiritual integrity, or oneness, is a common theme throughout Scripture, with metaphors such as marriage and the Trinity illustrating the call to be one. Isaiah wrote that God will rejoice over Israel as a bridegroom rejoices over his bride (62:5). The Old and New Testaments speak of apostasy as "adultery." The apostle Paul wrote of the mystery of "two becoming one" in marriage and the church.

Jesus prayed that the church might be one, linking our oneness with each other to the unity of the Godhead:

> . . . that all of them may be one, Father, just as you are in me and I am in you. May they also be in us so that the world may believe that you have sent me. I have given them the glory that you gave me, that they may be one as we are one: I in them and you in me. May they be brought to complete unity to let the world know that you sent me and have loved them even as you have loved me. (John 17:21–23)

The apostle Paul echoed Jesus' prayer when he urged the believer to be "like-minded," literally "of one mind" or "of one accord" (see Philippians 2:2, 20). Oneness is a frequent admonition and description in the writings of Paul.[3] The biblical call is for the church to be "harmonious in soul, in tune with Christ and with each other. . . united in thought and feeling . . . like clocks that strike at the same moment."[4] Paul writes, "Let this mind be in you which was also in Christ Jesus . . ." (Phillipians 2:5 NKJV).

Integrity is broken whenever a thought or act places personal interests above the interests of others. When people separate themselves from others they begin to think and act in ways that deny the lordship of Christ. This invites sin and separation.

When Jesus is Lord, leaders are no longer condemned to work out salvation by personal power or in secrecy. The church is neither surprised by sin nor fearful to admit failure. When made aware of sin, the sinner rushes into the light of others, where the sin can be confessed and forgiven, and steps for restitution and restoration may be worked out. Integrity acknowledges lordship and rushes sin out into the light.

We rarely expose our sin in the church because most of us are self-protecting and self-governing. Sin is a private matter. To protect feelings we keep sin in the dark. Rather than submit to a redemptive process of open confession and restoration, we cling to our rights and reputations. In raw terms, we lack spiritual integrity.

Why Go to Church?

Let's return again to the simple question, "Why do you go to church?" Most Christians we have interviewed have never thought about this question, assuming the answer was obvious. When forced to frame an answer, most fumbled for an adequate response.

Two reasons stand out. People say they go to church either out of habit or to meet a personal need. Rational (or "right-hand") believers hope to know more. Emotional (or "left-hand") believers hope to feel better. Typically each wants it in a three-point sermon or five easy steps. An interesting dynamic unfolds as the interview progresses: Hearing themselves speak, most realize what they are saying lacks integrity. Their words are hollow and inadequate—something far less than what the church is supposed to be. Still they rarely have an answer that satisfies, one that has purpose or meaning beyond themselves.

Do we know what the church is for? This is a theological problem that we will come back to in the next chapter. For now, two summary points should be made:

1. Conflict is always a complex interaction of cultural, structural, spiritual, and theological forces. Most conflict surfaces and displays interpersonal symptoms that have underlying systemic, theological roots.

2. The theological problem stated above is the deepest root. Theology drives all the others. All church conflict is ultimately theological. God wants to change the way we think about the church so that we might become His people.

What about your church? As you read the descriptions above, which dynamics of conflict do you see present in your situation?

Like frozen water pushing under the surface of a road, the only way to resolve and redeem church conflict is to identify its spiritual, cultural, structural, and theological roots; and then to address them. Pray that God will reveal what lies under the surface in your church.

Notes

1. This term was coined by Jay Forrester, who created the field of system dynamics.
2. Notice John 17; Ephesians 4:12.
3. Romans 12:1–5; 15:5–7; Ephesians 2:14–16; 3:6; 4:4–6, 25.
4. Philippians 2:2, Robertson's *Word Pictures in the New Testament* © 1930; as cited in Ken Hamel, *The Online Bible,* version 2.5.2 (Oakhurst, N. J.: Online Bible Software, 1995).

TOWARD A THEOLOGY OF RECONCILIATION

This is what the Lord says: "Stand at the crossroads and look; ask for the ancient paths, ask where the good way is, and walk in it, and you will find rest for your souls. But you said, 'We will not walk in it.'"

~ JEREMIAH 6:16

As we learned in chapter 1, most leaders use either a right-handed or left-handed approach to diagnose and address church conflict. Each perspective is useful in moving people toward reconciliation, but ultimately each is inadequate. Let's look at these two perspectives more closely.

THE "RIGHT-HANDED" APPROACH: EMPHASIZING TRUTH AND MIND

The right hand has long been associated with power and order. It is a symbol of knowledge, force, discipline, and truth. Those whose theology stresses the omnipotence and sovereignty of God tend to approach church conflict as a struggle for truth.

If you come from this worldview, you may have found yourself responding in anger and dismay to conflict and personal sin. You may think, *The problem is the loss of biblical obedience and adherence to truth. Of course conflict will result when the church panders to a sinful culture.* The church's tacit agreement with modernity before, and post-modernity today, has undercut the truth of the Gospel and bred a shallowness of faith that compromises the veracity of Scripture.

Right-handed responders believe that what the church needs most is to recover an appropriate fear and respect for a holy God. This can be accomplished best through expositional preaching, church discipline, and a renewed commitment to God's Word. Believers will be transformed as they are "sanctified by truth" by the "renewing of their mind."

This is the first common approach. There is another.

THE "LEFT-HANDED" APPROACH:
EMPHASIZING LOVE AND METHOD

The left hand, in contrast to the right, is associated with relationship and openness. It is the symbol of mercy, intuition, creativity, and love. Those who stress God's loving-kindness tend to approach church conflict as an opportunity to accept, forgive, and love the sinner.

If you are sympathetic to this worldview, you probably share the same alarm and dismay about conflict and sin as your right-handed brothers, but with rather different assumptions and solutions. For you, the alarm is not our unwillingness to attack culture but our failure to lovingly engage it. You conclude, *Conflict will result whenever a church is not a safe place for sinners to admit failure, be loved and forgiven.*

The church should be a place that welcomes sinners in order to save them and change them. Those who practice the left-handed approach believe the issue is not preaching or teaching about sin; everyone knows adultery and lying are wrong, for instance. Rather, the problem is the church's failure to acknowledge the power of forgiveness to overcome human sin. We must engage the world around us with the transforming power of God's love.

Left-handed responders do not endorse sin, but they believe the solution must be more than chastising the sinner. After all, who among us is without sin? The best approach is to explore and emphasize new ways to communicate God's forgiveness and acceptance of the sinner.

Left-handed believers seek to reach the lost by addressing the needs of our world openly and honestly. In some churches this means the use of media, drama, and music to attract unbelievers. In other churches this means focusing on building relationships through small-group fellowships and thematic or issue-oriented Bible study.

RIGHT VERSUS LEFT

The differences in right- and left-handed approaches have themselves become the cause of conflict in many churches—surfacing in any number of issues from political involvement to style of worship to principles of church discipline.

For instance, right-handed leaders tend to have an objective view of Scripture and a propositional or rule-based way of looking at life—if you do this, this will happen. Discipline and decision-making is typically autocratic and authoritarian, usually limited to one individual or a small group.

Left-handed leaders tend toward a more subjective, relational, or democratic view of life. They are concerned about legalism, so they emphasize love, mercy, fairness, and tolerance. Decisions are made by consensus or congregational vote.

Neither right nor left would discount the view of the other entirely. No one would dismiss the need for truth or for love. But each gives preference to one way of thinking and responding over the other.

Perhaps you are experiencing this tension now. Which do you prefer, truth or love? Is God right-handed or left?

IS GOD LEFT-HANDED?

Robert Farrar Capon, in his book *The Parables of the Kingdom*, recalls Luther's reference to God's "left-handed" power. Capon suggests that God is more left-handed than right.

Unlike the power of the right hand governed by the logical, plausibility-loving left hemisphere of the brain, left-handed power is guided by the more intuitive, open and imaginative right side of the brain. Left-handed power is paradoxical power: power that looks for all the world like weakness, intervention that seems indistinguishable from nonintervention.[1]

Capon challenges us to see that God often acts in unsuspecting, left-handed ways.

In fact, the more one insists on God's right-handed omnipotence, the greater our wonder at His restraint. When the world could have—and by all accounts should have—been blown to smithereens through the past four millennia, God did not do so. Why not?

Israel wanted the promise immediately; God waited two thousand years. They looked for a conquering king; He sent a baby born in a feed trough, who went on to die on a cursed cross.

Indeed, the life of Jesus looks like a miserable failure if you measure accomplishment by right-hand power. This rubs some of us the wrong way. We expect God to throw us a high heater, and He throws us a "long slow curve."[2] God appears more apt to choose the foolish and the weak of the world to shame the "wise" and "strong" (1 Corinthians 1:27).

Yet neither Scripture nor God fits neatly in a left-handed box. Just ask Korah and his followers (Numbers 16) or Ananias and Sapphira (Acts 5). Jesus is lamb and lion. He was compassionate with sinners and condemning of the Pharisees. The One who was silent before His accusers was overturning tables just days before. Jesus healed diseases, caused the blind to see and deaf to hear, cast out demons, and raised the dead with right-handed power. The apostles, at first amazed when "even the demons submit" to them in Jesus' name (Luke 10:17), would go on to perform miracles as well. Throughout Scripture, we find God invading or suspending His creative order with right-handed power. Indeed, the story is not over. It is impossible to read Revelation without seeing God's right hand.

So, is Capon right that God is left? How are we called to respond to conflict in our lives and churches?

The problem, of course, is the choice.

Winston Churchill talked about the need for *both* left- and right-handed power, addressing the world in another time and circumstance. That the world is always at war, Churchill said, is:

> *all the fault of the human mind being made in two lobes, only one of which does any thinking, so we are Right-handed or Left-handed; whereas, if we were properly constructed, we should use our right and left hands with equal force and skill according to circumstances. As it is, those who can win a war well can rarely make a good peace, and those who could make a good peace never win.*[3]

This aptly describes much of our confusion and struggle in churches. The aggressive win at the expense of fellowship, while the passive cannot lead through conflict.

What should be our approach? Do we root out sin and discipline the sinner to preserve the truth? Or do we forgive and forget to proclaim God's love?

The biblical witness points to a God who both uses and transcends right- and left-handed power.

ON BECOMING WHOLE

Right- and left-hand approaches are both necessary, yet, in themselves, still inadequate. They are necessary because each one addresses fundamental weaknesses and failures in the church.

It is true, the church has been far too tolerant and accepting of pagan culture. We have lost a sense of the holy. It is also true that the church has often been unloving and irrelevant. Right and left approaches are both inadequate because each emphasizes the individual, not the church. In fact, the church is hardly necessary for either.

Right-handed people are convinced that knowledge and mastery of God's Word is all that is needed, and that giving and receiving love is a "second-hand" concern. Left-handed believers see the application of truth as personally revealed and privately applied by the work of the Holy Spirit.

Each presumes that the hands are ours, not connected to a body of many other parts. We must recover the life-transforming work of God's Word and Spirit operating in and through the gathered community.

The arena of living out our call to truth and love is the church—God's people. The church is the only place in the world where the truth and love of Christ can lead to *shalom*—the Hebrew word for peace, which literally means "wholeness."

To be whole always requires others. There is no peace without the Holy Spirit speaking God's truth and revealing Jesus' love in and through the church, the body of believers.

These three—God's Word, His Spirit, and His people—are all necessary for the church to be the church that is redemptive.

God calls the church to be whole. We must learn to balance and move beyond objective, ultimately coercive legalism on the right hand, and subjective, ultimately passive relativism on the left hand.

Instead, the church must faithfully embody and practice salvation as a way of life. We must come to see that reconciliation is not something we simply know or even do. It is who we are. Nor is it reserved for those occasional times of conflict. Rather, reconciliation is a constant pursuit of holiness—a way of thinking, acting, and being that forms us in the church as it changes our collective character, habits, and practices.

LORDSHIP AND SUBMISSION

In every conflicted church, two or more factions are anxious to tell their story. The primary motivation of each is to make sure others know what is already obvious to them—that they are right and the other side is wrong.

Often I will say something like the following to a church so divided: "If you need to know who is right and who is wrong, our answer is simple. We are all wrong."

Church conflict is never about who is right and who is wrong. It is about lordship and submission; it is about a people who have stopped being the body of Christ. We stop being the church whenever we believe that we are capable of making ourselves. This is idolatry—the sin of Israel and of the church throughout history.

Scripture teaches that as Christians, we are shaped by God's Word, His Spirit, and His people. In my experiences with many church conflicts, most church members affirm the first two—the Word and the Spirit—but minimize or ignore the third—the church. This theological issue is at the crux of most church conflict.

As we discovered in the last chapter, our theology has been infiltrated by the values and virtues of popular culture. Our culture celebrates those who make themselves—people who work hard, rise above, and "pull themselves up by their own bootstraps." For many of us, our aim is to build self-esteem and to reach "our full potential."

Many churches unwittingly preach these values through a spiritual filter. Most pastors would never claim that we can make ourselves. God, of course, is our Creator. But we readily use language that at least implies autonomy and affirms individualism. We speak of faith as "a choice," "a journey" each person works out privately. Jesus is our "personal" Lord and Savior. We urge people to practice disciplines such as a personal quiet time. Sin is a private matter.

Many Christians fervently believe that if they diligently study God's Word and earnestly seek God's Spirit—alone—they will be changed. But they are not changed. Growth is incremental at best. Rare is the personal victory over a besetting sin.

The reason this is so is that we have lost a biblical understanding of our sin and God's work of salvation. This is a theological problem, the result of misguided assumptions and conclusions about what sin is and does, and how God has provided the answer through His Son and Spirit.

THE CHRISTIAN CONCEPT OF SIN AND SALVATION

The Bible describes sin in three ways: as forensic, ethic, and dynamic.[4] Let's look at each description.

FORENSIC: A LEGAL STATUS

The first way Scripture defines sin is in forensic, or legal, terms. The word *forensic* means a "legal argument" to be used in, or appropriate for, courts of law or for public discussion. A forensic laboratory, for instance, uses science or technology to investigate facts and establish evidence in a court of law.

In God's court of justice, all people are sinners. We are, all of us, declared guilty. This was not always so. We were created without sin and declared by God to be "good." With the fall of Adam and Eve, sin entered the world, changing our status before God from "good" to "guilty." (More on the Fall in the next chapter.) As Romans 5 declares, "Sin entered the world through one man, and death through sin, and in this way death came to all men, because all sinned" (v. 12). All mankind shares the same legal status of guilt from birth, as David proclaims in his psalm of confession: "Surely I was sinful at birth, sinful from the time my mother conceived me" (Psalm 51:5).

Question: How do we know this? Answer: By the law.

The apostle Paul tells us that God's law was established so that we might be made aware of our sin. "Therefore no one will be declared righteous in his sight by observing the law; rather, through the law we become conscious of sin" (Romans 3:20). The law establishes a standard against which we have fallen short. We are guilty, and God has found us out. Sometimes we are so deceitful and dishonest with ourselves that it takes a standard, or law, to make us aware of our sin. The law was given so that we might see ourselves and our need truthfully.

This is why Christian community is often so necessary and so uncomfortable for many people—because *true Christian community uncovers the sin in our lives.*

When confronted with the truth of our sin—our legal status before God—we feel guilt and shame. We are aware that we have no right, no status for relationship with a holy God. Forensic sin declares our separation.

ETHIC: "MISSING THE MARK"

Secondly, Scripture refers to sin in ethical terms as "missing the mark." The word *ethic* speaks to character, a set of principles and practices governing the conduct of a person. If forensic sin speaks about what we are, ethical sin speaks of who we are as revealed by how we think and what we do.

Ethical sin speaks of our character: our pride, our corrupted judgment, our self-centeredness, our inadequacies of various kinds that lead us into sin and failure.

Like one missing a target, the believer fails to become or to accomplish what God has called him to be or do. Sin has so invaded and corrupted our character as individuals that even when you and I have the desire to do what is good, we cannot carry it out. (See Romans 7:18.)

Ethical sin makes us aware of how badly we have missed the vision that God had set before us. We say with the apostle Paul, "What a wretched man I am!" (Romans 7:24)

Ethical sin speaks to our thoughts, habits, and practices that comprise our character. Here, sin acts to destroy our relationship with God and with one another.

DYNAMIC: THE POWER OF EVIL AND DEATH

Finally, Scripture speaks of sin as a spiritual dynamic. The word *dynamic* relates to power, ability, or energy. A dynamic is an inter-active system or process of competing or conflicting forces.

Scripture describes dynamic sin as a power that is external to us, seeking to defeat us. Dynamic sin is a spiritual battle involving prin-cipalities and powers that wage war against the believer. For some, dynamic sin is an addiction or habitual response that controls and overpowers a person. It is a pathway of destruction that can result in illness, even death.

Romans 6 describes us as slaves held in bondage to the powers of sin. (See vv. 13–14, 16–17, 20–22.) Dynamic sin is about the power of Satan to defeat, enslave, and control us.

ABOUT JUSTIFICATION, SANCTIFICATION, AND GLORIFICATION

The church must announce a gospel that addresses and recon-ciles these formidable powers of sin. The church must proclaim a gospel sufficient not only to forgive our sin but to transform our character. Reconciliation demands transformation. The Gospel of Jesus Christ must provide a salvation that is past, present, and future.

And so it does . . . through the welcome doctrines of justifica-tion, sanctification, and glorification.

JUSTIFICATION

The doctrine of justification declares that Christ died for our sins as a substitute for our guilt and shame. Upon repenting of our sin, we are forgiven, declared "not guilty"; Jesus Christ died that we might be free from our legal guilt. "God made him who had no sin to be sin for us, so that in him we might become the righteousness of God" (2 Corinthians 5:21). This work is confirmed by the Holy Spirit, who seals the believer for eternity. (See 2 Corinthians 1:22; Ephesians 1:13; 4:30.)

But salvation is not for legal status alone. Christ came that we might have abundant life. The apostle Paul tells us that God "chose us in him before the creation of the world to be holy and blameless in his sight" (Ephesians 1:4). We are called to live "worthy" of our faith. Salvation must be a present reality as well as a legal judgment. God wants to transform our character as well as save our soul.

SANCTIFICATION

Whereas ethical sin seeks to have us miss the mark, and to destroy us, Jesus called us into a new way of thinking and living. L. Gregory Jones reminds us that Jesus has called believers to "embody" as well as claim forgiveness from sin:

> *In the face of human sin and evil, God's love moves toward reconciliation by means of costly forgiveness. Human beings are called to become holy by embodying that forgiveness through specific habits and practices that seek to remember the past truthfully, to repair brokenness, to heal divisions, and to reconcile and renew relationships. . . . Learning to embody forgiveness involves our commitment to the cultivation of specific habits and practices of the Church. . . . The Christian life is learned and lived through the cultivation of specific habits and practices of forgiveness in the service of holiness that enable us simultaneously to unlearn our habits of sinfulness.[5]*

The Cross is formative and transformative. Here, as we shall see time and again, the church is absolutely necessary for claiming and living into our faith. The apostle Paul declared in Ephesians 2: 8–10 that our salvation is a free gift of grace. "We are God's workmanship," he wrote, "created in Christ Jesus to do good works, which God prepared in advance for us to do." (v. 10)

Grace can never be earned but must always be "worked out." We work out what God has put in. As Paul noted, "Therefore, my dear friends, as you have always obeyed . . . continue to work out your salvation with fear and trembling, for it is God who works in you to will and to act according to his good purpose" (Philippians 2: 12–13). Here, the term *work* does not mean that salvation and sanctification are up to each person to work harder in or pray harder about. Ethical sin calls for a different kind of saving than from forensic sin. Character is not transformed by obeying rules or by conforming to laws.

Rather, God would redeem our character through brokenness. We are to present ourselves as "living sacrifices" (Romans 12:1). We are transformed as we invite God to speak into our lives through His Word, His Spirit, and His church. It is the conscious, intentional submission of our thoughts, habits, and practices before the light of biblical truth, asking God to reveal our sin and to transform our character.

So Jesus prayed for His disciples, "My prayer is not that you take them out of the world but that you protect them from the evil one. They are not of the world, even as I am not of it. Sanctify them by the truth; your word is truth" (John 17:15–17). To "sanctify" literally means to "make pure" or to "clean up." God's Word cleans us. Sanctification is a corporate act of submission and obedience.

GLORIFICATION

Finally, whereas dynamic sin wants to control and enslave us, truth frees and empowers. The power of sin is broken by the Gospel, the announcement and proclamation that Jesus Christ is Lord. Here, Scripture describes a salvation that is future, as well as past and present.

My message and my preaching were not with wise and persuasive words, but with a demonstration of the Spirit's power, so that your faith might not rest on men's wisdom, but on God's power. (1 Corinthians 2:4–5)

Then the end will come, when he hands over the kingdom to God the Father after he has destroyed all dominion, authority and power. (1 Corinthians 15:24)

Since the children have flesh and blood, he too shared in their humanity so that by his death he might destroy him who holds the power of death—that is, the devil. (Hebrews 2:14)

To the Ephesian believers, Paul described a spiritual conflict between "rulers, . . . authorities [and] powers" of this dark world and "spiritual forces of evil" in the cosmos (6:12; see also 6:10–13). To the church at Corinth, he explained, "The weapons we fight with are not the weapons of the world. On the contrary, they have divine power to demolish strongholds" (2 Corinthians 10:4). Against these powers, God provides truth, righteousness, peace, faith, "salvation and the sword of the Spirit, which is the word of God" (Ephesians 6:17; see also 6:13–16). Believers are called to live into Christ's resurrection power, both now and for eternity. "By his power God raised the Lord from the dead, and he will raise us also" (1 Corinthians 6:14).

All this is for the praise of Christ's glory.

He raised him from the dead and seated him at his right hand in the heavenly realms, far above all rule and authority, power and dominion, and every title that can be given, not only in the present age but also in the one to come. (Ephesians 1:20–21)

Therefore God exalted him to the highest place and gave him the name that is above every name, that at the name of Jesus every knee should bow, in heaven and on earth and under the earth, and every tongue confess that Jesus Christ is Lord, to the glory of God the Father. (Philippians 2:9–11)

We ended chapter 1 with a question: "Do we know what the church is for?" Let's answer that question: The church is the realm where forgiven saints live into the Gospel. The church forms our character into Christ's image. Conflict tests and proves our character and our commitment to the Gospel.

Sin, Salvation, and Church Conflict

Of great importance is how we address sin within the church. In many approaches to church conflict, the leaders and members display a fundamental theological flaw: We tend to objectify sin. That is, we tend to identify and address sin as a violation of a moral law that has independent existence apart from the community, from our common relationship or experience. Righteousness is earned or lost by our ability to keep the law.

With this understanding of sin as forensic alone, we claim some forensic remedies, failing to recognize or address the ethical and dynamic natures of sin.

While visiting the West Coast one autumn, my wife and I drove along the picturesque northwestern Oregon coastline. On every beach, signs warned against swimming and wading in the surf because of "sneaker" waves—powerful waves that "sneak" onshore, catching unsuspecting waders and swimmers in a strong undertow.

But these waves also can frustrate would-be kayakers. One afternoon at lunch we watched an inexperienced kayaker attempt to paddle out from the shore. The waves were frequent and powerful. The kayaker was persistent and dedicated, paddling furiously between waves. But each new wave knocked the kayaker back to where he had started.

We began rooting for the kayaker, hoping he could conquer the waves. He tried for nearly an hour but never reached the crest of a wave before it broke and pushed him back to shore.

Many churches unintentionally advise members to approach sin in a similar fashion. Caught in cycles of failure or secret sin, they are told by the leaders to pray more or try harder. So the sinner fails, feels remorse, asks forgiveness for sin, and accepts God's grace. He applies rules and tries harder not to sin, only to fail and feel guilty once again.

The sinner goes to church week after week, fighting phases of guilt and confessing waves of remorse. He responds to altar calls and asks people to pray for him in hope that "if I just do more [or study more . . . pray more . . suffer more] for Christ, I will find victory and personal fulfillment." Hard as he tries, the cycle repeats itself over and over again.

As long as sin is addressed as a law, an event, or a condition outside of ourselves, we will continue to fail. Besetting sin is more than a bad decision; it is habitual, a part of our character. Unconfessed sin in the body of Christ can become a spiritual stronghold.

To be reconciled, we must proclaim the power of the Cross over our thinking and our habits—over the ethical and dynamic as well as the forensic nature of sin. As members of a local body of believers, we must nurture forgiveness and restoration rather than encourage greater sin and conflict. God would have us be reconciled in and through the church, not as individuals.

As we will see in the following pages, most church conflict is not about personal forensic sin, but about systemic ethical failure. *Church conflict is about character.* To redeem character we must be a community of faith being saved and sanctified together in mutual submission under Word and Spirit.

WALKING WITH CHRIST IN A LOCAL COMMUNITY

God would have us become His people. The Old and New

Testament Scriptures tell us that our character is formed by a "walk"—
a peculiar set of habits and practices learned and shared in a faith
community.

WALKING TOGETHER

The word for *walk* in both Greek and Hebrew carries the notion
of "life." A walk is a way of life. For the believer this way of life follows an "ancient path," grounded in God's salvation history. God
called out Abraham and separated for Himself a nation. In the fullness of time, the Father sent His Son to die on the cross and be raised
from the tomb, releasing the promised Holy Spirit, who was poured
out on Pentecost to establish the church. Requisite to Israel and to
the church is a people, a community. *The walk requires others.*

Note, for example, how each reference to "walk" in the verses
below is plural. These instructions and descriptions are written to
the church—to an incarnational community—not to individuals.

> If we claim to have fellowship with him yet walk in the darkness, we
> lie and do not live by the truth. But if we walk in the light, as he is in
> the light, we have fellowship with one another, and the blood of Jesus,
> his Son, purifies us from all sin. (1 John 1:6–7)

> And this is love: that we walk in obedience to his commands. As you
> have heard from the beginning, his command is that you walk in
> love. (2 John 6)

> It gave me great joy to have some brothers come and tell about your
> faithfulness to the truth and how you continue to walk in the truth. I
> have no greater joy than to hear that my children are walking in the
> truth. (3 John 3–4)

> The nations will walk by its light, and the kings of the earth will bring
> their splendor into it. (Revelation 21:24)

Several points can be made about how God seeks to change us. First, God wants to form us among a community of believers. God created us as social, spiritual beings. We are formed, for good and bad, by the culture and community we keep.

Second, our character is shaped as we submit our lives in common life and confession, sharing convictions that spring from a common story. The Christian story, of course, is embodied in the life, death, and resurrection of Jesus Christ. We are changed—transformed—as we submit to one another under the lordship of Jesus.

This begs a set of questions we must ask about ourselves:

~ *What is our story?*
~ *What kind of people is our story forming?*
~ *Do we look like a people under the lordship of Jesus Christ?*
~ *Does the fruit of our lives point to the Cross?*

If we find in our churches, for instance, acts of sexual immorality, impurity, discord, jealousy, selfish ambition, factions, or envy, we must ask ourselves, "Where does this come from?" What is it about us that sin is so prevalent?

When the apostle Paul wrote to the Corinthian and Galatian churches about fighting, dissension, and sexual perversion, he was not addressing personal sin but corporate failure. This is not what the church should look like. These churches were off track spiritually and theologically—adapting the values of a culture opposed to the Way. Paul wrote to warn them that they were learning to walk in the wrong direction.

THE RUTS THAT FORM US

The root for our English word *learn* originates with the Latin *lira*, a noun meaning "track or "furrow." To learn literally means gaining knowledge or understanding by following the same track. In other words, we learn in the "ruts" or tracks of the story we live by.

Faith is a long walk in the same direction.

The call of Jesus Christ in Scripture is for the church to be a separate people—living as aliens within a peculiar culture. The church is to be a contrast to the world around it—a culture to itself—different from the world in kind, purpose, and value. Indeed, those outside looking in should marvel at what is possible when a people live in community under the lordship of Jesus. Is this what people see looking in on your church? If not, why not?

The Greek word for church is *ekklesia*, a compound word with the prefix *ek*, meaning "out of," and the root word *kaleo*, meaning "called." *Church* literally refers to a people who are called out and called together.

This understanding of community is fundamental and primary to any theology of the church. We are called together into a story that stands in marked contrast to our world and contemporary culture. This contrast is not merely in what we know or even believe. It is who we are. We must recover and renew our ancient ruts.[6]

PAUL'S VISION FOR THE CHURCH

Remember our definition of the church and its purpose: "The church is the realm where forgiven saints live out the Gospel." In his letter to the Ephesians, the apostle Paul adds to our understanding of the purpose and function of the church. In Ephesians we find Paul's unvarnished vision for what the church is and what we are called to be.

A NEW RACE

Nine times in the book, Paul uses the word *ekklesia*, the Greek word for church.[7] The church, wrote Paul, is Christ's body, the spiritual and physical manifestation of His lordship on earth. This body is not a collection of individuals but one people, called out and into a new race proclaiming a new order. He described the purposes and dynamics of this unified body: "[Christ's] purpose was to create in himself one new man out of the two, thus making peace, and in this one body to reconcile both of them to God through the cross, by which he put to death their hostility. He came and preached peace to you who were far away and peace to those who were near" (Ephesians 2:15–17).

The church is "built on the foundation of the apostles and prophets, with Christ Jesus himself as the chief cornerstone. In him the whole building is joined together and rises to become a holy temple in the Lord," Paul noted. He concluded, "And in him you too are being built together to become a dwelling in which God lives by his Spirit" (2:20–22).

Paul described a world divided into two groups of people: Jews and Gentiles. To Jews living in the first century, a person was either Jewish or a dog, a Gentile. There was nothing in between. A great wall of hostility separated the Gentiles from any relationship with the Jews. To the Jews, the Gentiles were pagans with no rights, no tolerance, no inclusion. Paul reminded the Gentile believers that they were once "separate from Christ, excluded from citizenship in Israel and foreigners to the covenants of the promise, without hope and without God in the world" (2:12). But the Jews also were alienated from God when they refused to recognize and accept Jesus as Messiah.

Into this hopeless, godless world, however, Jesus came. His death and resurrection tore down the dividing wall. Jesus Himself became peace. Out of two different peoples He made one people (see 2:13–18). Note, however, that Gentiles did not become Jews and Jews did not become better Jews. Rather, Paul described a whole new race of people—a "people of the Way" (Acts 19:23; 24:22). Now in Christ, Jew and Gentile, Greek and barbarian, have become a people who gather reconciled under the lordship of Jesus Christ (Ephesians 3:6).

This reconciliation is both spiritual and relational, vertical and horizontal. In Christ we are reconciled not only to God but to one another. We live and prove the power of the Cross through living out our reconciliation.

A Prayer for Unity

When Jesus met with His disciples in the Upper Room just hours before His betrayal, He washed their feet, predicted His crucifixion, and promised the Holy Spirit. Jesus urged the disciples to remain attached to the vine, promising joy that would come out of grief. Then Jesus prayed—for Himself to be glorified; for His disciples to be sanctified by truth; and for all who would believe down through the centuries to be brought to complete unity. Jesus prayed that we would be one so that the world would see the truth claims of the Gospel in us.

Paul picked up this same theme in Ephesians, describing the church as the bride and body of Christ, a holy people unified in "one Lord, one faith, one baptism; one God and Father of all" (4:5–6). This oneness is essential to the integrity of the church. The apostle stated clearly God's intention for unity: "His intent was that now, through the church, the manifold wisdom of God should be made known to the rulers and authorities in heavenly realms" (3:10). The heavens marvel in praise to God when the church is the church.

A Life Worthy of the Calling

Having set out these doctrines in chapters 1 through 3 of his letter, Paul exhorted the Ephesians "to live [into] the calling you have received" (Ephesians 4:1).

In effect, Paul said, "I beg you to live a life worthy of the church." We are to conduct our lives in a way that is worthy of our calling. The word *worthy* is *axios,* meaning "weight." It is the same root for our English word *axiom.* Literally, it means balancing equal parts so both sides are true, or leading a balanced life, your actions being consistent with your words.

We might say it this way: Make your walk equal to your talk; or, live a life that looks like the faith you are called into. Note it is "the calling you have received." That is to say, our calling to Christ and to the church is not something we accomplish alone or live up to. We receive our calling by grace through the Holy Spirit.

Our calling is not something we possess, but a life we live into. We must not live *up* to our calling, which is individualistic and event driven. Living *up* to our calling is striving that is temporary and inadequate. It is conforming—changing from the outside in. It is reactive, not generative. It is worship without lordship, fellowship without brotherly love, service without sacrifice.

Living *into* the Gospel, in contrast, is an ongoing "walk" with others. It is an inside-out spiritual discovery process in which God's Word, His Spirit, and His people combine to form and transform us. The body lives and grows and proves the calling together.

Salvation joins sanctification. As believers "work out their salvation," they grow in sanctification. Being saved is not merely a ticket out of hell. It is an invitation into a way for life. It is past, present, and future. Paul, throughout his writings, spoke about salvation interchangeably as a past event, a present reality, and a future hope—the "already, but not yet."

That is, we live into our salvation by joining others in a specific way of hearing, seeing, thinking, acting, and being. The church becomes the place—the spiritual space—where God's redemptive purposes take place.

A WORKING DEFINITION: THE CHURCH

To capture this idea about what it would look like to live worthy of our calling, we return once more to our working definition of the church: "The church is the realm where forgiven saints live into the Gospel." A brief explanation of key words will help clarify what we mean.

CHURCH

The church is comprised of a people called out by God, in Christ, through the power and active, indwelling presence of the Holy Spirit.

We are a called-out, called-together people.

REALM

The church is a space, not a building or a place. It is the "social construction of a spiritual reality"[8] that owes its life, purpose, and identity to the lordship of Jesus Christ.

We belong to a kingdom that is worldwide and forever—a salvation story that is many thousands of years old and coming to a certain end. The church is the visible form of this kingdom here and now, and yet to come, what theologian George Eldon Ladd has called "the presence of the future."[9] That is, we live in the "in-between" times,[10] as residents of a present-imperfect, yet future, Perfect Kingdom. In Christ, the church lives as an earthly gathering of a coming, heavenly kingdom.

FORGIVEN

The basis of our coming together is not that we are good or knowledgeable people, but that we are sinners saved by grace. As saints, we do not stop being sinners. The difference between a pagan and a believer is not the absence of sin but the application of God's atoning sacrifice to confess, be forgiven of, and change our sinful habits.

As forgiven sinners, we will sin, the apostle John wrote (see 1 John 2:1–6). But if we are careful to obey and honest to confess, we can form new habits of righteousness and walk, more and more, as Jesus did. It is in confession that we identify failure and commit to change those habits of thought and action that lead to sin. In confession, the church gathers as sinners at the foot of the cross.

SAINTS

Sinners still, we are, together, being saved by Jesus Christ and sanctified by the Holy Spirit. Salvation and sanctification are past, present, and future realities that God is working out in the church, the community of the forgiven.[11] We are participants in a narrative that is leading inexorably to an end, the consummation and judgment of all in Christ.

LIVE INTO

We are sojourners living into a coming kingdom. By "into" we mean both participating in and working out God's redemptive plan. The kingdom is not static, something we merely locate ourselves "in," nor do we live "out" the kingdom as if we had any power over it. The Gospel announces a salvation that we live "into." Until Christ returns, God calls men and women to grow redemptive communities reflecting His grace and peace. The church is the place where we work out our salvation through commitments and confessions that form new habits that change our lives, that develop Christlike character.

GOSPEL

We embody the Good News that now, in Christ, there is peace. The church is a cruciformed people (that is, formed and transformed by the Cross) who gather together in mutual submission to celebrate, proclaim, and practice the life, death, and resurrection of Jesus Christ.

The church is the organic, generative, and life-giving force into which every believer is called. It is not a machine. The church is not something we can manufacture or control. It is a body; more than that, it is Christ's body. We have no right or claim to be part of this body apart from the grace of Jesus Christ.

In Christ's body there is no room for self. Jesus Christ is the subject and object of all things.

When we grasp this truth—as we must—then and only then does the church become what God intends. We no longer go to church to have our needs met or our brains filled. We go to church to meet and to submit to the One who is Lord over all.

Notes

1. Robert Farrar Capon, *The Parables of the Kingdom* (Grand Rapids: Eerdmans, 1985), 20.
2. Ibid., 15.
3. William Manchester, *The Last Lion: William Spencer Churchill Alone, 1932–1940* (Boston: Little Brown, 1988), 27.
4. In this brief study of sin I am indebted to conversations with, and unpublished writings by, my friend David Fitch, Ph.D.
5. L. Gregory Jones, *Embodying Forgiveness: A Theological Analysis* (Grand Rapids: Eerdmans, 1995), 49.
6. See Robert E. Webber, *Ancient Future Faith: Rethinking Evangelicalism for a Postmodern World* (Grand Rapids: Baker, 1999).
7. See Ephesians 1:22; 3:10, 21; 5:23–24, 25, 27, 29, 32.
8. This phrase is used often by my friend and co-laborer in Christ, David Fitch.
9. See George Eldon Ladd, *The Presence of the Future* (Grand Rapids: Eerdmans, 1974).
10. Gordon Fee, *The First Epistle to the Corinthians,* F. F. Bruce, ed., *The New International Commentary on the New Testament* (Grand Rapids: Eerdmans, 1987), 16.
11. Stanley Hauerwas, *A Community of Character* (South Bend, Ind.: Univ. of Notre Dame, 1981).

Three

LEADING AND FORMING BIBLICAL COMMUNITY

*After beginning with the Spirit, are you now trying to
attain your goal by human effort?*
~ GALATIANS 3:3

In the previous chapter we discovered how God desires to form
us in and through biblical community. We are a called-out, called-
together people.

But what does this mean? How should it change who we are and
what we do in the church? What kind of leadership would be
required?

Pick up almost any book about church growth or leadership
today, and the dominant theme will be performance—how you can
do more and achieve more. Words like "effective," "dynamic," and
"productive" describe the values and goals of leadership. Much is
given to models and methods of leadership and growth. Little is said
about spiritual formation.

We would do well to ask ourselves the same rhetorical question Paul posed to the Galatians: "After beginning with the Spirit,

are you now trying to attain your goal by human effort?" (3:3). Consider this verse in the context of your church.

- Is your church performance-based or Spirit-formed?
- Are you trying to attain your goal by human effort or by the empowering presence and leading of God's Spirit?
- What would have to change for your church to become a Spirit-formed community?
- How do your goals shape your practice?

A Spirit-formed community has a new identity, reality, and activity.

A NEW IDENTITY

A Spirit-formed community is formed by the life, death, and resurrection of Jesus Christ, not the personality or gifts of a man or woman.

When a church gathers around a central figure who leads out of his or her knowledge, experience, or gifts alone, the church's identity is inevitably tied to the ego and self-esteem of the leader. It becomes performance-based. By performance-based, we mean that planning and evaluation are focused on human achievement. Success or failure is measured by the growth and size of the church, the number of conversions, the latest facility expansion, or whether people approve of sermons, music, and so forth. Identity is measured by position, power, and accomplishment.

Note that the focus of performance is on a man, not God. Few pastors would admit that the identity of their church is tied to their ego or is being formed in their image. But many churches are being shaped this way with at least the passive permission of their pastors.

For instance, how do people describe your church? A red flag should go up in our minds whenever people refer to their church by the first or last name of the senior pastor. "I go to Bob Smith's church."

Leaders who fall into this category generally do leadership alone. Paul addresses this in his first letter to the Corinthians:

> My brothers, some from Chloe's household have informed me that there are quarrels among you. What I mean is this: One of you says, "I follow Paul"; another, "I follow Apollos"; another, "I follow Cephas"; still another, "I follow Christ." Is Christ divided? Was Paul crucified for you? Were you baptized into the name of Paul? (1 Corinthians 1: 11–13)

To the Galatians, Paul said what amounts to this: "Don't be an idiot. (See Galations 3:1–4) You did not start in your own strength. Don't finish that way." It is not about you, your performance, or your self-esteem.

Rather, our identity as leaders and members must be in Christ crucified. "I have been crucified with Christ and I no longer I live, but Christ lives in me," Paul declared (Galatians 2:20). In the Spirit-formed community our identity is changed from self (whether our collective self or personal self) to that of the Cross.

Instead of gathering around the personality and gifts of a central leader, instead of going to church to boost my self-esteem, have my needs met, or increase my knowledge, I gather with brothers and sisters in mutual submission to the lordship of Jesus Christ. We meet one another at the foot of the Cross, becoming the body of Christ, a living witness to what is possible when people live into the life, death, and resurrection of Jesus.

When the church is formed around self-esteem, we condemn our members to live lonely, powerless lives, each one trying to grow in human strength. In biblical community, by contrast, believers grow up together as all submit to the truth of Scripture and to the operation of God's Spirit to and through one another.

So, while our identity changes, our reality changes also.

A New Reality

When a church is performance-based, human nature guides our concerns. We succumb to the values and methods of the secular culture around us—consumerism, humanism, narcissism, and individualism. This understanding of reality is based upon *self*-understanding and *self*-expression. It is conformity. We look like the world. We are like the world.

In a community of contrast, reality is based upon and formed around a Spirit-nature, where the church is a holy space. This agent is the Holy Spirit working in and through the believer (personal) and church (corporate) to "clean," or make holy.

Sanctification is linked to and follows naturally from salvation. In the church, salvation and sanctification are gifts to be lived, not commodities to consume. Righteousness is not a possession but something I live into. In the gathered community, something becomes possible by the empowering presence of God's Spirit that is not possible anywhere else on earth. Here we are transformed, made new, by God's Spirit.

As we are made new, as our identity and our reality change, our activity changes also.

A New Activity

In a performance-based church, the activity is performance. We use tools, laws, methods, and rules to cajole and coerce activity. We entertain, persuade, and perform.

Ministries in worship and preaching are measured by "what I got out of it." People think *I feel good,* and conclude it must be good worship. Performance-based churches spend an inordinate amount of time creating, planning, and promoting ways for people to be involved in activities with minimal commitment. They do this, they believe, because they are in competition with the everyday demands of work schedules, soccer practices, and personal family time (not to mention other churches).

Busyness is both a common excuse and a leading rationale for why pastors and staff must create ever-new and exciting ministries. When attendance declines in an evening or midweek service, the common explanation is "our lives are so busy." (For example, in 2001 our ministry served eight churches in various parts of the United States, each of which insisted that its region was "more busy" than the rest.)

Busyness is a value of a performance-based world, not a Spirit-led community. This becomes clear when we are reminded of God's call for a Sabbath rest: "There are six days when you may work, but the seventh day is a Sabbath of rest, a day of sacred assembly. You are not to do any work; wherever you live, it is a Sabbath to the LORD" (Leviticus 23:3).

God wants to redeem our view and use of time. Busy people, like all people, always do what they perceive is most valuable. A performance-based view of activity measures time and success as a commodity to be attained. We are what we consume. So we speak of "spending," "wasting," or "using" time as if it were ours to control.[1]

Against this notion stands a community that measures who we are and what we do by holiness, not effectiveness. In the church, God is seldom in a hurry. He is leading, perfecting, and changing us like apprentices under the tutelage of a master. Christianity is a craft that must be learned over time, a discipline with specific habits and practices that we grow into, guided by God's Word, His Spirit, and one another.[2]

Over and against rules and methods, our activity must be shaped by truth and grace. Instead of being governed by laws, we're governed by the fruit and gifts of His Spirit.

Our character is shaped not by trying harder alone but by making and keeping commitments with one another through confession, repentance, and forgiveness.

All we do is governed by a new understanding of our identity as a cruciformed people and a new reality where God, by His Spirit, makes of us a "chosen people, a royal priesthood, a holy nation, a people belonging to God, that [we] may declare the praises of him who called [us] out of darkness into his wonderful light" (1 Peter 2:9).

SPIRIT-FORMED LEADERSHIP

A Spirit-led church must have Spirit-formed leadership. Here again, the Scriptures describe leadership one way while most churches operate another. The Bible outlines a body diversely gifted and empowered, working collaboratively. Leaders are servants who embody God's vision, define current reality, set and keep boundaries, nurture community, and feed the flock. Such leaders are shepherds who keep watch over as well as equip the flock (Acts 20:28).

Further, Scripture distinguishes between positional authority (the role or title of a leader) with spiritual authority (God operating through call, gifting, and character).

Performance-based leadership emphasizes position and power. In contrast, the priority of Scripture is placed on servanthood, gifts, and character. A classic illustration of the difference between performance-based and Spirit-formed leadership is given to us in John's gospel:

An argument developed between some of John's disciples and a certain Jew over the matter of ceremonial washing. They came to John and said to him, "Rabbi, that man who was with you on the other side of the Jordan—the one you testified about—well, he is baptizing, and everyone is going to him." To this John replied, "A man can receive only what is given him from heaven. You yourselves can testify that I said, 'I am not the Christ but am sent ahead of him.' The bride belongs to the bridegroom. The friend who attends the bridegroom waits and listens for him, and is full of joy when he hears the bridegroom's voice. That joy is mine, and it is now complete. He must become greater; I must become less." (John 3:25–30)

The difference between performance-based and Spirit-formed leadership is in the identity of the leader—as performer versus servant.

Put yourself in John's sandals. The Baptist was the first on the block to baptize. There was only one John the Baptist. So John's disciples came to him and said, "This upstart, Jesus, is taking away your market share." John's disciples needed John to be great. In a performance-based understanding of the church, the image of pastor or leader is everything. For some, it is carefully scripted to be humble and caring. In others, the pastor must be seen as a superhero. In either, he must be greater than his competition.

The Baptist's reply is instructive: "He must become greater; I must become less."

Where is your joy? Who is the object and subject of your ministry? How supportive are you of the other evangelical churches and ministries in your region? Is there competition or cooperation? Performance requires measurement and comparison. "If one church has a praise band, we must have a better one, or, if we cannot compete here, we must have a better youth or singles ministry."

THE LEADER AS SUPERHERO

When the church becomes a platform for supersaints, it becomes a theater, not a church.

Several years ago I heard a story told about Muhammad Ali, the former heavyweight boxing champion, that reveals the false claims of a superhero.

The champion was aboard a commercial jet about to take off on a transcontinental flight. The flight attendant came down the aisle and, noticing that Ali's seat buckle was not fastened, said, "Please buckle your seatbelt. We're about to take off."

Ali replied, "Superman don't need no seatbelt," to which the flight attendant responded, "Superman don't need no airplane."

The church does not need superheroes, nor does God create them. We create them at great peril to our leaders and our churches. The proper perspective every pastor and lay leader should have is given in 1 Corinthians 3:4–6:

When one says, "I follow Paul," and another, "I follow Apollos," are you not mere men? What, after all, is Apollos? And what is Paul? Only servants, through whom you came to believe—as the Lord has assigned to each his task. I planted the seed, Apollos watered it, but God made it grow.

God gives the spiritual growth, not men.

THE LEADER AS SERVANT

Over and against the superhero, the Spirit-formed leader is first and foremost a servant. This leader starts with the assumption that God needs him or her for nothing. We serve at the pleasure and gifting of our Lord. It is all grace.

Note the contrast between performance-based and Spirit-formed leadership styles in the chart on the next page. God's Word calls leaders to stand in marked contrast to the world.

Several years ago, I was presenting this material at a pastors conference in Texas. During a break in the session, a young man came up to me and said, "I'm sick."

"I'm sorry to have this effect on you," I apologized.

"No, no," he responded, "I'm sick because *I am* all those things you described as performance-based . . . and the seminary that I'm going to is training me to be that way!"

Have you been taught or bought into a performance-based model of ministry? Instead of forming churches around one leader, we need to build churches around the collective gifts of a Spirit-formed community.

To lead a church into the character of God will require leaders who form and are formed by the life, death, and resurrection of Jesus Christ. To be the kind of community that forms people around God's character, we need a way of hearing, seeing, thinking, and acting informed by God's Spirit.

PERFORMANCE-BASED VERSUS SPIRIT-FORMED LEADERSHIP

The performance-based leader . . .	The Spirit-formed (servant) leader . . .
has to have all the answers.	continually asks questions. His or her assumption is "I don't know the truth completely, but by God's grace we can discover, obey, and grow together."
has to be certain.	lives by faith with uncertainty.
has to control.	facilitates learning and growth.
operates as a symbol that takes center stage.	is a model who points to Christ and gets out of the way.
is easily threatened by others who know or who can do more, and he in turn threatens others because his identity is based upon keeping his own image or performance.	empowers others to grow and to serve.
looks at events, measures mistakes, and hides his faults for fear of being exposed.	looks for underlying structures that are causing patterns of problems. He or she is willing and ever ready to confess sin.
typically works alone.	builds an interdependent team.
will measure and demand authority by title or position: "I am the pastor" or, "I have a doctorate."	follows a call and practices gifts for the glory of Christ—"I must decrease."

A Change of Mind

The Greek word for *repent* in Scripture is *metanoia*. It literally means to "change your mind." We need to change our thinking, to recover what it means to gather together not as individual consumers competing to meet needs or gain knowledge, but as a "holy nation," a redemptive community that gathers in mutual submission to Jesus as Lord.

How can leaders begin to train their people and grow their church in redemptive community? We must learn to think and to act historically, redemptively, communally, interdependently, and eternally.

THINKING AND ACTING HISTORICALLY

Every year our ministry with churches, named appropriately enough Metanoia, holds several learning retreats for young pastor couples to foster spiritual and leadership formation. Each time we gather, a different couple share the story of the church where they serve.

Often the pastor-couple will begin their story at the founding of the church. "It all started back in 1997 . . ."

Following their presentation, the group will ask questions about joys and hardships—mile markers in the life and heritage of the church. We encourage the church to mark God's activity through celebrations and rituals that recall the past.

At some point I will ask the pastor couple why they started their story in "1997."

They look at me puzzled and reply, "Because that's when our church started."

Then I will lead them through a series of questions and answers, such as:

"But your church is part of a denomination, right?"

"Yes."

"And the denomination is more than one hundred years old, correct?"

"Yes."

"Does your denomination follow an even older, greater theological tradition?"

"Yes."

"And that tradition takes its authority from the Scriptures?"

"Yes."

"New Testament or Old?"

"Both."

"So when should your story really begin?"

"About 4,000 years B.C. . . ."

For many pastors—young and old—this is a new way of thinking. A church that forms itself around God's character must tell the full story. We must learn to place ourselves in a continuum of God's salvation history. Without a salvation history greater than our contemporary experience, needs, or minds, we are stuck with self-made notions about reconciliation. We must locate our identity in a narrative much larger than ourselves.

This will remind us of God's greatness and our smallness. We start the story with Abraham, and by the time we get to our church we have a healthy view of what makes us important—God's grace, not our works.

God knew us before the creation of the world. Our God is the God of Abraham and Isaac and Jacob. We stand in a long line of men and women who through trial and persecution passed down a faith that has demonstrated itself truthful through thousands of years. We belong to a calling that links us with the saints in Hebrews 11, who, even now, the writer to the Hebrews tells us, look on as "a great cloud of witnesses" (Hebrews 12:1).

What is your church story?

THINKING AND ACTING REDEMPTIVELY

The story that is ours in Christ is a salvation story. That is, we must grow people who come together first and foremost as sinners who found deliverance by the sacrifice of Jesus.

This is the message of Jesus in the Gospels. It is the message of Paul throughout the Epistles. We are sinners saved by grace. Our ability to hear, to respond to, and to be changed by Jesus is directly related to our ability to see ourselves as sinners.[3] This is the point of the parable of the lost sheep, the lost coin, and the prodigal son. Lostness was the requirement for being found. We have been found and claimed by the redemptive act of Christ at Calvary.

THINKING AND ACTING COMMUNALLY

From the beginning of Creation when God said, "It is not good for the man to be alone" (Genesis 2:18), until the coming consummation of time, man was made for others. The church is a called-out people. Everything we do in the church is shaping people, either into a body that looks more like Christ or into consumers who look like the world.

> But you are a chosen people, a royal priesthood, a holy nation, a people belonging to God, that you may declare the praises of him who called you out of darkness into his wonderful light. Once you were not a people, but now you are the people of God; once you had not received mercy, but now you have received mercy. Dear friends, I urge you, as aliens and strangers in the world, to abstain from sinful desires, which war against your soul. (1 Peter 2:9–11)

The church is God's agent for reconciliation and spiritual transformation. God created us for Himself and for one another. Jesus prayed for us to be one even as the Father, Spirit, and Son are one. In the Trinity, there is no competition, only mutuality and reciprocity.

The assumption of the New Testament is that salvation and discipleship are located in the church. The Gospels and Epistles always assume a common life and fellowship of believers. Church is not a place we go to but a life we live into—a life worthy of our calling. This implies faith wants others.

The Christian is formed in and through the church as believers gather in mutual submission to God's Word, His Spirit and to one another. This theme is noted throughout Scripture and described specifically in the New Testament "one another commands." One-another commands are reciprocal, mutual commands. The apostle Paul uses the phrase *one another* repeatedly to describe the church as a people who are intimately connected as members of Christ's body. To be a follower of Jesus is to belong to others. Paul writes, "In Christ we who are many form one body, and each member belongs to all the others" (Romans 12:5).

Twenty-eight verses in the New Testament provide guidance for

HOW TO LIVE WITH ONE ANOTHER

Our Attitudes	**Our Commitment**
Accept one another (Romans 15:7).	Confess sins and pray for one another (James 5:16).
Be at peace with one another (Mark 9:50).	Forbear one another (Ephesians 4:2).
Be devoted to one another (Romans 12:10).	Forgive one another (Ephesians 4:32).
Be kind to one another (Ephesians 4:32).	Greet one another (Romans 16:16).
Belong to one another (Romans 12:5).	Live in harmony with one another (Romans 12:16).
Encourage one another (1 Thessalonians 5:11).	Wait for one another (1 Corinthians 11:33).
Fellowship with one another (1 John 1:7).	Wash one another's feet (John 13:14).
Have equal concern for one another (1 Corinthians 12:25).	
Honor one another (Romans 12:10).	
Love one another (John 13:34).	
Be humble with one another (Romans 12:16).	
Our Work	**Our Warning**
Admonish one another (Colossians 3:16).	Do not judge one another (Romans 14:13).
Carry burdens for one another (Galatians 6:2).	Stop grumbling with one another (John 6:43).
Instruct one another (Romans 15:14).	Stop passing judgment on one another (Romans 14:13).
Offer hospitality to one another (1 Peter 4:9).	
Serve one another (Galatians 5:13).	
Speak truthfully to one another (Ephesians 4:25).	
Spur one another toward love (Hebrews 10:24).	

how believers are to live with one another. As shown above, we should relate to each other in our attitudes, commitment, and work, while recognizing the warnings against division.

The one-another commands are the pathway to holiness. As a church learns to practice and to embody the one-another commands, character is transformed. Salvation and sanctification become a way of life. Such actions toward others will transform not only our churches but our marriages, our child-raising, and our work. Our relationship to the world will also change as the church bears witness to God's grace and justice through preaching and caring for widows, the poor, and those in prison. We learn a new way of seeing and thinking about our needs, seeing them as God does, and meeting them as He does—in Christ through one another.

THINKING AND ACTING INTERDEPENDENTLY

The model of Old and New Testament leadership is interdependence. God called Moses *and* Aaron, kings *and* priests, prophets *and* judges. Jesus called twelve disciples and sent them out, two by two. The apostle Paul traveled and led in teams of two or three, equipping bands of fellow workers wherever he went. For example, notice his use of "we" in 1 Thessalonians 1: "Our gospel came to you not simply with words, but also with power, with the Holy Spirit and with deep conviction. You know how *we* lived among you for your sake. You became imitators of us and of the Lord" (vv. 5–6, italics added).

The principle of Scripture is that wisdom and strength are found in interdependence, mutual submission, and common purpose—in teamwork. We are not a redundancy of parts under one head, but a body. Each part is valuable and purposeful.

This is not how we've been trained. We equip individuals, not teams; teach monologue, not dialogue; focus on knowledge, not character; measure performance, not faithfulness.

Churches formed around the personality and skills of a pastor set up our churches and our pastors for failure. It is madness.

Engulfed by unreasonable expectations and overwhelming demands, a pastor must decide between autocratic control or democratic tolerance. Neither is biblical. Neither is leadership. Neither has power to address and correct our culture's never-ending consumer appetite.

Consider, for example, the epidemic of church conflict over worship style. Listen to the views and arguments expressed, and you will quickly learn that the debate is framed around individual preference, making the consumer in the pew, not our Father in heaven, the object and subject of the worship planning. The pastor who imposes a solution or asks for a vote fails to lead.

Rather, the church needs leaders who will teach and guide believers into worship that makes the character of God and the work of Christ the object and subject of all word and song. Worship is the gathering of sinners in mutual submission under the lordship of Jesus Christ.

THINKING AND ACTING ETERNALLY

The church is an eschatological (future-focused) community. We are the "already, but not yet" community of faith that proclaims and practices a future hope not yet realized. Like the men and women of faith celebrated in Hebrews, we participate in and we welcome a story that looks to an eternal end: "All these people were still living by faith when they died. They did not receive the things promised; they only saw them and welcomed them from a distance. And they admitted that they were aliens and strangers on earth" (11:13).

We are strangers and aliens to earth because we were made for eternity. As Paul wrote, "If only for this life we have hope in Christ, we are to be pitied more than all men" (1 Corinthians 15:19).

Even as church leaders must help their people think and act historically—looking backward—leaders must give equal attention to what lies ahead. The church must be ever pointing to the Alpha and Omega, the beginning and the end.

With this brief theological foundation to guide us, we can now look at how God would have us anticipate, prevent, and reconcile conflict in the church.

Notes

1. Philip Kenneson, *Life on the Vine* (Downers Grove, Ill.: InterVarsity, 1999), 116–17.
2. Stanley Hauerwas, "Discipleship as a Craft, Church as a Disciplined Community," *The Christian Century*, 1 October 1991, 881–84.
3. Stephen E. Fowl, *Engaging Scripture* (Malden, Mass.: Blackwell, 1998), 81.

WHY ALL CONFLICT IS ABOUT LEADERSHIP

A Christian psychologist recently told me that she was going to stop accepting Christians for counseling. When I asked her why, she gave three reasons: "Because Christians do not want to get well, their identity is linked to being sick, and they want everything for free."

"Sounds like most of the churches we work with," I replied.

As I meet Christians around the country and I'm asked about our ministry to conflicted churches, a common first response is, "You should come to my church." Conflict, it seems, is everywhere in the evangelical church. For some, it has become part of their identity.

In the following chapters we will explore how our response to conflict can actually make our conflicts much worse. Our first response is usually wrong. It is a negative, learned response.

Typically we choose one of four primary conflict response

styles: passive, evasive, defensive, or aggressive. Each style is negative because it falls short of biblical peacemaking principles. Each style will lead to frustration and failure because it is self-centered, based upon self-protection or self-promotion. Each exchanges biblical truth and love for self-truth and self-love.

Your conflict style has much to do with your personality and the family system or culture you grew up in. From your earliest days you learned how to cope with and protect yourself from conflict. Usually, these are unconscious patterns of thinking and behaving that are hard to break.

These chapters will help you understand how God wants to change your habits of thinking and responding to conflict. You will see yourself in one or more of the negative styles. But I want to be clear; our purpose is not to better understand and accept ourselves. Our purpose is repentance—a "change of mind." Your conflict style is evidence of sin, not individuality. It is the arena where you will tend to sin most often—against God, others, and yourself—when conflict emerges. And, of course, each of us sins.

Recognizing and owning your negative response style is the first step to understanding your part in conflict, and how your response may actually be making the conflict worse. Knowing your style will help you discover how you need to change your mind and behavior in present and future conflicts.

But first, we need to define what we mean by church conflict.

Four

A BIBLICAL VIEW
OF CONFLICT

*Peacemakers who sow in peace raise a harvest of
righteousness.*
~ JAMES 3:18

Most Christians hold false notions about conflict. Those false
notions follow their right- and left-handed views of God and the
church.

Left-handed believers (those who see God as all-loving and who
want to emphasize acceptance and forgiveness) typically discourage
any thought or talk about conflict for personal or privacy reasons.
*Conflict, they reason, is sin, the result of human rebellion in the Gar-
den of Eden. Therefore, all conflict is bad.* Left-handed believers often
want to be positive and loving at all times. Peace is kept by avoiding, denying, or running from conflict.

Right-handed believers (those who see God as omnipotent and
who want to emphasize truth and authority) typically view conflict
in terms of power. Conflict is about control. For these, conflict is
necessary to "separate the sheep from the goats," to defend or pre-

serve sound doctrine, and to prove who is right and who is wrong. Right-handed believers are often quick to point out how they have insight, authority, or anointing that others do not possess. Right-handed leaders keep peace by reactive, defensive, and aggressive responses.

Both positions above have some basis in Scripture. Human conflict is surely a consequence of sin. But not all conflict is sin. Further, as we shall see at the end of this chapter, peace is something we make, not keep.

Conflict is God-purposed. The conflict in your life right now is not a surprise to God, nor beyond His power to work out for good purposes. God allows conflict, perhaps even leads us into it, that we may know His love and trust His peace.

Peace is God-provided. Spiritual conflict existed prior to the Fall, cosmically preceding humanity, when Satan fell from heaven due to his rebellion. (See Jesus' words in Luke 10:18.) Adam and Eve's disobedience brought humanity into the battle. By God's grace, spiritual peace is provided in Christ, now and forever.

CONFLICT AND THE CHURCH

Paul described the church as God's agent to unfold His redeeming plan: "His intent was that now, through the church, the manifold wisdom of God should be made known to the rulers and authorities in the heavenly realms. . . . For our struggle is . . . against the rulers, against the authorities, against the powers of this dark world and against the spiritual forces of evil in the heavenly realms" (Ephesians 3:10; 6:12).

Where you start influences where you arrive. If you begin with a notion of avoiding sin on the left hand or defending doctrine on the right, the full discovery of God's redemptive purpose is lost. A redemptive view of conflict requires a full biblical view.

Guarding truth is vital. Paul gave clear instructions to Timothy and Titus to "hold firmly to the trustworthy message as it has been taught, so that [they] can encourage others by sound doctrine and refute those who oppose it" (Titus 1:9).

A trustworthy message requires the church to keep its trust. Holding a trust does not mean control, however. In fact, what Paul seemed to encourage in Timothy he also criticized in the Pharisees. What was the difference?

Paul followed Jesus in teaching that knowing doctrine is secondary to being faithful. It is not the letter but the spirit of the law that man must follow. This is at the root of most of the conflict between Jesus and the religious leaders of His day. Jesus' life and actions challenged, reinterpreted, and sometimes contradicted the accepted doctrine or orthodoxy of the Pharisees. He ate with sinners and healed on the Sabbath. He pronounced forgiveness—something only God could do. Jesus broke the rules. The Pharisees elevated the literal words of the law above the incarnation of the Word.

This may be a sobering lesson for those who today follow the Pharisees when they elevate knowledge of the Word above submission to one another. This is spiritual arrogance, not holiness.

WHAT DOES SCRIPTURE SAY ABOUT CONFLICT?

Conflict, James wrote, springs from the need-based, self-absorbed attitudes and actions discussed earlier. Consider his inspired ("God-breathed") words in James 4.

What causes fights and quarrels among you? Don't they come from your desires that battle within you? You want something but don't get it. You kill and covet, but you cannot have what you want. You quarrel and fight. You do not have, because you do not ask God. When you ask, you do not receive, because you ask with wrong motives, that you may spend what you get on your pleasures. You adulterous people, don't you know that friendship with the world is hatred toward God? Anyone who chooses to be a friend of the world becomes an enemy of God. Or do you think Scripture says without reason that the spirit he caused to live in us envies intensely? But he gives us more grace. That is why Scripture says: "God opposes the proud but gives grace to the humble." Submit yourselves, then, to God. Resist the devil, and he will flee from you. Come near to God and he will come near to you. Wash your hands, you sinners, and purify your hearts, you double-minded. Grieve, mourn and wail. Change your laughter to mourning and your joy to gloom. Humble yourselves before the Lord, and he will lift you up. (vv. 1–10)

Conflict is the result of unwarranted and unfilled desire. It is unwarranted because the desire is for personal pleasure and self-promotion, not for understanding or seeking God's will. It is unfulfilled because our motive, like our desire, is self-seeking.

It may be that we breeze over these words quickly, letting ourselves off easy with human desire. After all, we are human. Friendship with the world is common. Is it really so bad?

Note, James calls this adultery. Throughout Scripture, selfish desire is likened to sexual misconduct. The prophet Jeremiah is even more graphic, comparing God's people to camels and donkeys in heat (Jeremiah 2:20–25).

We dare not take desire lightly. It is at the heart of all conflict.

UNDERSTANDING THE WORD "CONFLICT"

Interestingly, the word *conflict* is assumed everywhere and stated almost nowhere in Scripture. In fact, the New International Version of the Bible translates the word only twice, once in each Testament:

Why do you make me look at injustice? Why do you tolerate wrong? Destruction and violence are before me; there is strife, and conflict abounds. (Habakkuk 1:3)

For the sinful nature desires what is contrary to the Spirit, and the Spirit what is contrary to the sinful nature. They are in conflict with each other, so that you do not do what you want. (Galatians 5:17)

In Galatians, the apostle Paul is describing a spiritual tug-of-war between the flesh and the Spirit. Each opposes the other. They are lined up in conflict, face to face, like two boxers. This echoes the spiritual battle in Ephesians 6. Here again, however, we need to receive Paul's words in the context of biblical community. This is not a personal contest—my flesh against my spirit—in which I try harder to be better. God's Word and Spirit are powerful but not sufficient, because they are not the full story.

Galatians, Ephesians, and the great majority of Scripture were written to and for God's people. God's remedy for this spiritual battle is not the Spirit and Word working through me to defeat my desire. The Word and Spirit must have a social and spiritual context in and through which the full work of God may be achieved. God's place for this is the church. It is in and through the people of God that the empowering presence of God's Spirit is released to lead us into truth; the power of the Spirit comes through spiritual gifts and spiritual fruit of brothers and sisters in whose company we mutually submit to declare the lordship of Christ over our sinful desire. As we walk in and by the Spirit *together,* we are forgiven, changed, renewed, and transformed.

It might be necessary for you to pause and process these words in the context of your personal life and struggles. Let me say it directly: Stop trying to save yourself. God does not require or intend for you to defeat desire by yourself. Trying to do so will lead you into conflict, not resolve it, no matter how diligent you are in private devotions and personal prayer.

OTHER WORDS FOR CONFLICT

Other words, such as *dispute, quarrel, strife,* and *contention* are used more frequently in Scripture to describe biblical conflicts.

In the Old Testament, the Hebrew word is *rib,* meaning a physical or verbal battle, indicating the presence of strife or a quarrel between two people. This word is used for admonition and warning repeatedly in the book of Proverbs; for example, "He who loves a quarrel loves sin; he who builds a high gate invites destruction" (17:19).[1]

In the New Testament, the Greek word for strife and contention is *eris.* The apostle Paul frequently warned leaders and the church against this sort of wrangling: "But avoid foolish controversies and genealogies and arguments and quarrels about the law, because these are unprofitable and useless" (Titus 3:9).[2]

In other New Testament texts, the military term *machomai* is used. Normally reserved for describing hand-to-hand combat, here the image is a war of words.

> Bear with each other and forgive whatever grievances you may have against one another. Forgive as the Lord forgave you. (Colossians 3:13)

> And the Lord's servant must not quarrel; instead, he must be kind to everyone, able to teach, not resentful. (2Timothy 2:24)

FIVE BIBLICAL TRUTHS ABOUT CONFLICT

From the verses above and the context of many other passages, five points can be made about church conflict.

1. CONFLICT IS A BROKEN RELATIONSHIP.

All conflict involves broken relationships. This includes relationships between humanity and God, humanity and others, humanity and self, and humanity with the created world (both this world and the cosmos).

Relationship implies a common life shared by a common language—the ability to communicate thoughts, actions, and feelings in truth and love.

In the Genesis account of Creation, the Garden is described as a paradise of perfect relationships. God spoke the world into being. "And God said, 'Let there be light,' and there was light" (1:3). Then God gave His inanimate creation identity through naming. God called the light "day," and the darkness he called "night" (1:5).

God spoke creatures into being and blessed them through spoken word (1:20–22, 24–25). Note, however, that God did not name the animals. Instead, man was created in the image of God and welcomed into the generative, creative process. God asked Adam to name the animals. "Now the LORD God . . . brought [the animals] to the man to see what he would name them; and whatever the man called each living creature, that was its name" (2:19).

Let this image sink in for a moment. Imagine God bringing each animal to Adam "to see what he would name them." Imagine the creative joy, the binding unity shared between God, man, and the creature as Adam describes and names each animal. "You are stately and bold; I will call you lion."

It is conjecture, of course, but one wonders whether the ability to communicate was limited to God and humanity. Could the animals speak also? Was there dialogue or understanding between the human and the creature? Eve does not seem surprised by the serpent's speaking to her. Genesis implys that God regularly strolled through the garden in the cool of the day. Did He converse with His created order?

Whether or not God's creatures were able to speak audibly or communicate with one another in the Garden cannot be known. What is clear, however, is a picture of harmony. Humanity was created for, and placed within, communion with God, with self, and with the plant and animal kingdom.

Lurking behind the scenes, however, was a war in the heavens. Having already been cast out of heaven, Satan now brought his cosmic war with God to the created habitants of earth. Note Satan's choice of warfare: not force, but cunning—a question of doubt.

Now the serpent was more crafty than any of the wild animals the Lord God had made. He said to the woman, "Did God really say, 'You must not eat from any tree in the garden'?"

The woman said to the serpent, "We may eat fruit from the trees in the garden, but God did say, 'You must not eat fruit from the tree that is in the middle of the garden, and you must not touch it, or you will die.'"

"You will not surely die," the serpent said to the woman. "For God knows that when you eat of it your eyes will be opened, and you will be like God, knowing good and evil." (3:1–5)

Sin was desiring equality instead of community with God. Sin broke community. Unity was replaced by enmity.

So the Lord God said to the serpent, "Because you have done this, 'Cursed are you above all the livestock and all the wild animals! . . .' To the woman he said, "I will greatly increase your pains in childbearing; with pain you will give birth to children. Your desire will be for your husband, and he will rule over you."

To Adam he said, . . . "Cursed is the ground because of you; through painful toil you will eat of it all the days of your life. It will produce thorns and thistles for you, and you will eat the plants of the field. By the sweat of your brow you will eat your food until you return to the ground, since from it you were taken; for dust you are and to dust you will return." (3:14–19)

Relationships once unified by love and nurture were now, due to sin, separated by hatred and hostility. Communion was broken in four places: between God and humanity, man and woman, human with himself or herself, and humanity with creation.

The gospel of Jesus Christ is the story of God's redemptive work to restore those broken relationships. God, in Christ, breaks down the wall of separation and hostility.

> For [Christ] himself is our peace, who has made the two one and has destroyed the barrier, the dividing wall of hostility, by abolishing in his flesh the law with its commandments and regulations. His purpose was to create in himself one new man out of the two, thus making peace, and in this one body to reconcile both of them to God through the cross, by which he put to death their hostility. (Ephesians 2:14–16)

Conflict is first and foremost a broken relationship. Reconciliation is the process of restoring broken relationships. This became possible in Christ, when "the Word became flesh and made his dwelling among us." (John 1:14)

2. CONFLICT IS A SPIRITUAL COLLISION.

While all conflict is about broken relationships, conflict in the church is not limited to people. There conflict is relational *and* spiritual. As we have already seen, believers are players in a cosmic battle. Remember, "Our struggle is not against flesh and blood, but against the rulers, against the authorities, against the powers of this dark world and against the spiritual forces of evil in the heavenly realms" (Ephesians 6:12).

All conflict is in some measure about spiritual warfare. Some churches are actively engaged and attacked by spiritual forces.

No church should minimize Satan's power or question his existence. But neither should we be afraid. The good news is that Christ is greater still and Lord over all. In the name of Jesus Christ and on the basis of His resurrection, the church is given authority to "drive out evil spirits and to heal every disease and sickness" (Matthew 10:1) and "to overcome all the power of the enemy" (Luke 10:19).

Most church conflict is not the result of demonic influence.

Pointing a finger at Satan has become a form of spiritual escapism, a convenient way to shift the focus from human responsibility to the devil.

Some spiritualize conflict through positive thinking. These folks believe that if we speak positive things, positive things will happen. So they say, "Forgive and forget," wanting to smooth over issues, making sin less than what it is. While we always must forgive and forget "what is behind" (Philippians 3:13), Scripture is also clear that true repentance, reconciliation, and restitution require a radical and complete "change of direction" and "change of mind." This means facing conflict directly and owning fault completely. We can never forget where we came from.

In the same way, there is a tendency among some to attribute to Satan what is more rightfully willful disobedience of men and women. The apostle Paul warned the believer: "In your anger do not sin: Do not let the sun go down while you are still angry, and do not give the devil a foothold" (Ephesians 4:26–27). This passage implies that whatever foothold the devil has is the likely result of our failure to keep short accounts of sin and our unwillingness to apply the blood of Christ and the power of the Resurrection over evil.

This is the case with most church conflicts. The public issue, or presenting cause, is often relatively small, insignificant, and not the real issue. Rather, conflict is usually a result of many suns going down on unresolved and unreconciled issues. As time passes and sins go unconfessed, the many footholds can make a stronghold.

When Metanoia Ministries is called into a church conflict to assess the issues, we bring an interdependent team of men and women. These are mature believers who are recruited and trained to discover and discern spiritual matters. The assessment is scheduled and planned weeks in advance. Prayer is a priority and a major emphasis of our work. Every team member has one or two people praying for him or her during the assessment weekend, and we commission a special intercessory prayer team to pray for us also. The church itself is called to prepare for the assessment by fervent prayer.

The result is that the Holy Spirit frequently reveals events and issues that are surprising and often unsuspected. Sometimes they come out in personal interviews where suddenly an image or idea comes to mind.

Once, while interviewing a married couple in a church, the woman (Jane) suddenly broke down in tears. I asked her what was wrong. She said that a memory had come to mind that had no apparent context to my question or our purpose.

"I'm sorry," Jane said, embarrassed. "This is silly. It has nothing to do with what we are talking about."

I suggested that it might be relevant in a way she could not see and asked her to describe what she was thinking. "No, I'd rather not," Jane said.

We went on with the interview. Minutes later, Jane interrupted the conversation again to say, "I have to tell you now."

Jane proceeded to tell us the story of a traumatic event from her early childhood. When she was twelve years old, a doctor touched her inappropriately during a routine examination. She had never told anyone about this before, including her husband, who was sitting with us in the room.

Why did this memory come to her mind during our conversation?

As we explored this question together, Jane said, "The feeling I had in the doctor's chair is the same feeling I have now in the pastor's office." Jane was careful to point out that the pastor had never touched her inappropriately, but the feeling of degradation was the same.

Our assessment team had already interviewed two hundred people in this church. A disturbing pattern had emerged concerning the pastor's attitude toward and treatment of women. This was a growing concern to us and a matter of prayer for confirmation. Jane's memory fit a pattern we had heard from many about the pastor's manipulative nature and abuse of power.

Was this God's purpose in bringing up a memory? Perhaps. It is not our purpose to investigate or prosecute church leaders. We rarely have all the facts completely or know the hidden forces at work. Much of life is mystery and is meant to remain this way, so we trust God for vindication and justice, not ourselves.

We did not include Jane's memory in our evidence, but we did receive her story as confirmation from the Lord. Later that weekend we recommended that the pastor resign immediately and submit to biblical counseling to explore his attitude toward women and to help reconcile the many hurts he had caused in the church.

Scripture is clear, and our work with conflicted churches has confirmed this many times: Church conflict is always spiritual. It is a spiritual collision.

3. CONFLICT IS INEVITABLE.

If all conflict is relational and spiritual, it follows that all Christians will face conflict. We are relational and spiritual beings. Conflict, like sin and death, is inevitable. We must deal with it.

The apostle Paul, in characteristic frankness, laid the problem out succinctly: "For the sinful nature desires what is contrary to the Spirit, and the Spirit what is contrary to the sinful nature. They are in conflict with each other, so that you do not do what you want" (Galatians 5:17).

Church conflict should not surprise us. We are sinners. We do not do what we know to be right, because we have competing desires caught up in a cosmic battle. We want to love God, but our love of self is strong. We want to be good shepherds, but we are not good. We are, all of us, conflicted. Rebellion flows through our veins.

I have seen this predisposition for rebellion more clearly—in myself and in the church—since moving to New Hampshire.

Our town was founded in 1776. Sixty-five people live in the village with three hundred or so dairy cows and a few dozen sheep. Like many old New England towns, the colonial church stands at the center of the common. Built by our forebears to be the gathering place to unify people in worship and everyday life, this church is little more than a historic landmark now. On a good Sunday, ten people will show up for services.

Our New Hampshire state motto is "Live free or die." We like clear cut options. The landscape is framed by rock walls, keeping out and hedging in desperately lonely and fiercely independent people. We mark out our lives with boundaries, warning others not to cross. Robert Frost penned his famous poem "The Mending Wall" from his New Hampshire farm. The poet described a neighbor, who wanting privacy, explained the reason for his fence: "Good fences make good neighbors."[3]

Remember the central notion upon which the United States was founded—independence. It is a nice word for rebellion. For two hundred years Americans have been building and keeping walls that define our autonomy. Most of our denominations and independent churches have followed the same pattern. We emphasize what separates us, not what unites. So, too, each of us has been brought up in—and bought into—a way of thinking that acts first and foremost for the benefit and defense of oneself. Many, like Frost's neighbor, believe in fences. It is the American way.

It is not God's way.

> You were separate from Christ, excluded from citizenship in Israel and foreigners to the covenants of the promise, without hope and without God in the world. But now in Christ Jesus you who once were far away have been brought near through the blood of Christ. For he himself is our peace, who has made the two one and has destroyed the barrier, the dividing wall of hostility. (Ephesians 2:12–14)

I lived for a period of time in a small rural area of the Adirondacks. In a town nearby, a Baptist church had split many years earlier over an issue that no one could remember. The resulting two churches struggled with a few dozen members, choosing independence and mediocrity over reconciliation and community. Each affirmed the Cross, but their very existence denied its power.

Issues that split churches range from the important to the ludi-crous—from disputes over doctrine to the color of the carpet. Our evangelical heritage is littered with petty conflicts.

In every conflict intervention, Metanoia has asked for a history of the church. A clear pattern has emerged. Most conflicted churches have unreconciled conflict in their past. The sins of one generation have been passed on to the next, and the next. Many times, the present leadership is comprised of people who formerly attended another church nearby where they failed or left unreconciled, bringing their unresolved issues with them.

More alarming is a common practice of many denominations to move pastors from one church to another without reconciling the past. (Remember Pastor Tim of "Second Church"?) It is not uncommon for denominational leadership to move a failed pastor out of one church and into another without telling either church why. It is wrong, but we do it anyway.

Rebellion is not news. Wherever there are people, even good people, there will be conflict. It is inevitable, until Christ returns.

4. CONFLICT IS NECESSARY.

One bright blue summer day a few years ago I stood outside a demonstration tent at the New Hampshire Craftman's Fair, fascinated with a blacksmith working iron. These demonstration tents are set up for public education. Different craftspeople take turns practicing their craft publicly, describing how they work and answering questions. In this tent, the smith was big and burly, as you would imagine he should be. He worked fast and focused, though with the freedom of one who knew his work. His task was forming a wrought-iron lampstand, undoubtedly something he had made many times before.

While he worked, the smith explained the process: how the iron must be heated to be twisted, then pounded evenly with a hammer against the anvil to mold the bends and curves. Just the right heat. Just the right pounding. Too little or too much of either would misshape the iron.

Carefully and with precision, the smithy pounded the iron and tapped the anvil—pound and tap, pound and tap. I understood the pounding, but why tap the anvil? The tapping, he explained, provides the rhythm so the pounding is even. With each tap the smith turned the iron slightly so the pounding did not weaken any one spot more than others.

As iron to the blacksmith's hands, so we are in God's.

Then the LORD said to Satan, "Have you considered my servant Job? There is no one on earth like him; he is blameless and upright, a man who fears God and shuns evil. And he still maintains his integrity, though you incited me against him to ruin him without any reason." "Skin for skin!" Satan replied. "A man will give all he has for his own life. But stretch out your hand and strike his flesh and bones, and he will surely curse you to your face." The LORD said to Satan, "Very well, then, he is in your hands; but you must spare his life." (Job 2:3–6)

"Simon, Simon, Satan has asked to sift you as wheat. But I have prayed for you, Simon, that your faith may not fail. And when you have turned back, strengthen your brothers." (Luke 22:31–32)

Did you notice that Satan had to ask permission to test Job and Peter? Are you in the heat of battle? Do you feel pounded? If so, think of the blacksmith who shapes the iron. "No temptation has seized you except what is common to man. And God is faithful; he will not let you be tempted beyond what you can bear. But when you are tempted, he will also provide a way out so that you can stand up under it" (1 Corinthians 10:13).

Satan may heat and conflict may pound, but only within God's rhythm, and never beyond what you may bear. God holds us—and molds us—in His hands.

As we have already learned, Scripture describes conflict as an inevitable, spiritual battle. "If you do not do what is right, sin is crouching at your door; it desires to have you," God warned Cain just before he rose up and murdered Abel. (Genesis 4:7) Now we discover that conflict is necessary for God's redemptive purpose. This is what the disciples could not understand that night in the Upper Room. "I have to go away," Jesus told them. But then He added, "I tell you the truth: It is for your good that I am going away. Unless I go away, the Counselor will not come to you; but if I go, I will send him to you" (John 16:7).

Jesus had to "go away"—to die—so we might live. Jesus had to go to the cross to defeat Satan once for all. Jesus had to go away that the Holy Spirit might come. Death. Crucifixion. Agony. Separation. All were necessary. All had to be endured for the "joy set before him."

Without sickness, we do not know health. Without evil, we do not know good. Without conflict, we do not know peace. Conflict is necessary for God to shape us.

5. CONFLICT IS AN OPPORTUNITY.

Margaret attended a church I served many years ago. Confined to a wheelchair for most of her adult life, Margaret lived with a body both contorted and misshapen, ravaged by multiple sclerosis. She spoke softly, often slurring her words in barely audible grunts. She drooled constantly and was in pain nearly all her waking hours.

Margaret had grounds for complaint; but she did not complain. She loved Jesus, and she never missed church. Sunday morning and evening, midweek prayer meeting, and special gathering, Margaret was always there, always in a neatly pressed dress.

One night, after I first arrived at the church, I was conducting a forum asking questions and facilitating dialogue with a group of about twenty people. I asked people to tell me their favorite Bible verse or a passage from Scripture that was personally meaningful.

Several people offered verses that I noted on a flip chart up front. (Whenever we work in conflicted churches we make a point to stay close to Scripture. God's Word is alive and active, binding us together as well as revealing and judging our thoughts [see Hebrews 4:12].)

After many people spoke, Margaret let me know she wanted to say something. Her friend interpreted her words for me.

"Margaret would like to share her life verse," the friend said.

"What is it?" I replied, welcoming her participation.

"Psalm 119:71," the friend replied.

Most of the people had recited their verses from memory or read them aloud from Scripture. Since Margaret could not speak, I looked up the verse for the group and read it for her: "It is good for me that I was afflicted," I read, "that I may learn Thy statutes" (NASB).

Margaret smiled broadly and nodded her head. Her wheelchair was a testimony to grace.

People like Margaret bring clarity and perspective. We want instant answers; God shapes eternal purposes. We see our temporal pain; God sees our eternal glory. "For momentary, light affliction is producing for us an eternal weight of glory far beyond all comparison" (2 Corinthians 4:17 NASB).

Joseph told the brothers who sold him into slavery, "You intended to harm me, but God intended it for good to accomplish what is now being done, the saving of many lives (Genesis 50:20). God's purpose for conflict is to accomplish redemption. Every conflict is an opportunity to work out our salvation according to God's redemptive plan. Our conflicts are God-purposed and always for good. As Paul wrote, "in all things God works for the good of those who love him, who have been called according to his purpose. . . . For I am convinced that neither death nor life, neither angels nor demons, neither the present nor the future, nor any powers, neither height nor depth, nor anything else in all creation, will be able to separate us from the love of God that is in Christ Jesus our Lord" (Romans 8:28, 38–39).

As we have seen, conflict is a broken relationship, a spiritual collision; it is inevitable and even necessary. Most of all, conflict is an opportunity to trust God for positive change—to make peace.

In the next few chapters we will explore four common negative responses to conflict: passive, evasive, defensive, and aggressive. Each response is common yet unbiblical, and it always leads us into greater conflict. As you read each chapter, ask God to reveal your thoughts, habits, and practices during conflict.

CONFLICT BENCHMARK

Before you continue, however, it will be helpful for you to think about an actual conflict in your life. This may be a conflict that you

---

A CONFLICT BENCHMARK

1. Present Conflict

You may be in conflict right now with a member of your congregation or a member of your board. Describe this conflict briefly below (or on a separate sheet of paper).

I am in conflict now with:

Specifically, we are in conflict because:

This conflict makes me feel:

To solve this conflict, I need help in:

---

2. Past or Repeating Conflict

You may have repeated conflicts with a spouse, child, in-law, boss, neighbor, or family member. Choose one repeating conflict and describe it briefly, using the statements below as a guide. If you do not have a present or repeating conflict, think about and describe a past conflict that you have faced.

A past or repeating conflict I face(d) is with:

Specifically, we are in conflict because:

This conflict makes me feel:

To solve this conflict, I need help in:

are presently facing or a recurring conflict that you are likely to face again in the near future.

In the space in "A Conflict Benchmark" (page 108), or on a separate piece of paper, jot down your thoughts in answer to the questions prompted.

We will use this Conflict Benchmark to measure, guide, and apply the principles in the following chapters.

Notes

1. The word *rib* also appears in the following verses: Proverbs 10:12; 13:10; 15:18; 16:28; 17:1, 14; 18:6; 20:3; 22:10; 26:17, 20–21; 28:25; 29:22; 30:33.
2. The word *eris* also appears in the following New Testament verses: Romans 1:29; 13:13; 1 Corinthians 1:11; 3:3; 2 Corinthians 12:20; Galatians 5:20; Philippians 1:15; 1 Timothy 6:4.
3. Robert Frost, "The Mending Wall," *The Poetry of Robert Frost* (New York: Holt Rinehart and Winston, 1969).

PASSIVE RESPONDERS:
WHY PEACEKEEPING IS NOT PEACEMAKING

---

*Then the LORD said to Cain, "Where is your brother
Abel?" "I don't know," he replied. "Am I my brother's
keeper?"*
~ GENESIS 4:9

Imagine you are in a board meeting discussing a difficult issue.
Roger, a vocal member of the board, is dominating the discussion.
He gives his opinion of what is wrong and how to fix it. Roger is confident, self-assured, and aggressive. He speaks often. People respect
his views and fear his temper.

As you listen to Roger speak, you become increasingly anxious.
You do not agree with his opinion, but you know the cost of challenging Roger. He is very competitive. Emotions might flare. He
might snap back. The meeting could end in another fight as meetings have before. Your friendship, tentative as it is, might be strained.

Still, you know that some of Roger's facts are wrong. He is mis-
stating or misunderstanding some important points. You even suspect that Roger might be intentionally leaving out some details. You
suspect that he may have a personal agenda in making his proposal.

As the boardroom discussion continues, the dissonance and disagreement build in your mind. The more you hear, the more you believe Roger is wrong. You can feel your blood pressure and body temperature beginning to rise. You are sure now that Roger is leading the board in the wrong direction.

You want to say something, but your mind is blank. The words simply will not come. Fear and doubt flood your mind. You hope someone else will speak up. Why don't others see what you see? Apparently, no one does.

Glancing across the table again you see Roger's determination to force his way. Everything in you says he is wrong. How can he say and believe these things? But with every urge for you to say something comes a greater wave of doubt and fear. *I may be wrong . . .* you think. Then you hear yourself saying, *Is this really worth fighting over? Maybe this is God's will.*

Discussion begins to wane, and you know the opportunity to ask a question or give an insight is ending. Still, you remain silent. Roger calls for a vote. "All those in favor say 'aye,'" the chairperson says. "All those opposed say 'nay.'"

In your heart you are screaming "Nay!" but you say nothing. The motion carries. No one notices that you did not vote.

Driving home from church, you are filled with competing emotions. You are mad at Roger for his suspect motivations. You begin to think of all the things you could have said but didn't. You can find the right words now, but it is too late. You are frustrated at yourself for not speaking out. Yet you quickly rationalize what happened, saying to yourself, *It would have been a big fight. It is better not to cause dissension.* As you pull into your driveway you breathe a sigh of relief, happy that you have kept the peace. You don't have to worry about conflict with Roger or other board members because no one knows how you feel.

If you identify with the story above, you are likely a person whose first response to conflict is passive. The following descriptions will help you understand more about how and why you respond passively and, more important, how God wants you to change.

A Definition and Description of Passive Responders

Webster's Revised Unabridged Dictionary defines *passive* as "not active, but acted upon; suffering or receiving impressions or influences; as, they were passive spectators, not actors in the scene." The word *passive* is Middle English, from Old French and Latin words meaning "subject to emotion" and "to suffer."

A passive responder will suffer greatly during conflict. Yet passive people have learned over time how to remain placid in great stress, often feeling great emotion but showing no outward or visible reaction to negative words or actions. Passive responders endure conflict inwardly, submitting to or remaining silent about a disagreement or offense.

People who use passive responses tend to believe that all conflict is wrong and must be endured quietly. Passive responders often are "left-handed" in their worldview. They believe mercy and love forbid any confrontation. They will go to great lengths to deny or rationalize feelings of anger and to avoid speaking the truth when it hurts. Passive responders are usually quiet, unassertive, compliant, nonresistant, and submissive.

Because maintaining relationship is their supreme value, passive responders will hold secrets and cover up truth to protect themselves or others from being hurt.

Passive Responders and Truth

In an effort to make a conflict go away, passive responders will surrender themselves, surrender relationships, and surrender the truth. Passive responders are more interested in keeping themselves and others from hurt than they are in reconciling themselves or others to God's truth. Their primary need is to be loved and accepted, even if that love comes at the expense of truth. Passive responders will pay almost any price to belong.

This left-handed approach to conflict is unbalanced because it holds a superficial, even selfish view of love. Such responders may tell themselves that their first concern is others, but their passivity is ultimately self-centered. Since it ignores truth, it is dishonest.

If you are a leader, passive responses can be devastating to your church. Scripture speaks about a leader's responsibility to keep watch, warning about the consequences of a passive response: "But if the watchman sees the sword coming and does not blow the trumpet to warn the people and the sword comes and takes the life of one of them, that man will be taken away because of his sin, but I will hold the watchman accountable. . . . So hear the word I speak and give them warning from me" (Ezekiel 33:6–7).

Silence is not golden in the church. Keeping silent is a passive form of lying. It is deceitful. Believers are called to speak the truth in love. Allowing false impressions about people or circumstances engenders more discord, not less.

Pretending the problem does not exist, denying personal responsibility, or refusing to face a problem directly abdicates the responsibility of being a brother or sister and the authority of being a watchman.

PASSIVE RESPONDERS AND FEAR

Why do some leaders find themselves keeping silent or passive in conflict? Fear.

Fear is the single greatest obstacle to most church leaders today. Passive responders are often overcome or paralyzed by fear—fear of their own judgment and the response of others. They fear rejection or disagreement. *What if they don't listen?* they worry. Fear causes doubt and second-guessing. *What if I am wrong?* they wonder.

The Book of Ezekiel makes clear the leader's role. The leader is called to report what he sees and hears, to warn the people. Note:

Leaders are not called to be right or to be certain. They are called to trust and to be faithful.

Further, the leader is not responsible for the response of others. He is called to warn. If the people listen, the leader has saved both them and himself. If the members fail to listen, the members are responsible for their own rebellion. But if the leader fails to warn, the leader is held accountable for his sin and the sin of all the people.

A Leader's Silence

A leader's silence is more than failure to lead. It is unbelief, even deceit. It doubts the power of God to redeem, reconcile, and intercede.

Ken pastored a small church. The church was struggling and losing members. When we met, it quickly became clear that Ken was a big part of the problem. He was a passive, wounded man.

In the course of our personal interview, Ken claimed his primary strength was in counseling and preaching. He admitted that he was "not a visionary, not an evangelist, not an up-front person, not a confrontationalist, and not a detail person." Ken's honesty and his willingness to be vulnerable was commendable, but his deficits were critical for any person in leadership.

It became clear that Ken's struggles were not new. He spoke several times about the "baggage" he brought to the church. When asked to elaborate further, he would not. We learned later that Ken had been fired from two previous churches.

A clear pattern emerged in our assessment of Ken's ministry. He tended to act toward others based upon how he perceived they would act toward him. If people liked or supported Ken, he tended to respond in kind to them. If not, he avoided initiating contact or ministry. This pattern was repeated in his counseling as well as visitation.

Some members loved Ken and spoke highly of how he had helped them through a personal family crisis. Ken had spent a great deal of time with these people, often going out of his way to care for them. Ken felt needed and loved.

But when others went to Ken with concerns about the vision and direction of the church, Ken shunned or ignored them completely.

Ken called on those who returned to him feelings of worth. He never visited or followed up with people whom he thought did not like him or appreciate his ministry. When people left the church, even people he was once close to, Ken would sever all contact.

As concerns about his leadership mounted, Ken took great pains to make everything look normal. At the same time, he avoided those who approached him with concerns about his preaching, the style of worship, need for follow-up visitation, and so on. Some members were bitter in their hearts and brutal in their attacks. But many other members and fellow leaders went to Ken with genuine love and concern. Ken responded the same to all who opposed him. He listened politely but never entered into dialogue or discussion. We found little or no evidence that Ken attempted to understand, address, and resolve the issues after they were brought to his attention. When it would have been easy for Ken to do something to help alleviate the concern, he took no action, going on with ministry as if no one had said anything.

Of course, Ken's reaction only frustrated church members even more. Their pastor, they thought, did not care. Of course, Ken cared intensely. Inwardly, he was deeply wounded. Outwardly, he displayed little or no evidence that there was a problem.

In the end, the conflict consumed the church, and Ken had to leave the pastorate. Months later, Ken still saw himself as a victim. In a sense, he was right. He was a victim of his own passive conflict-response style. But Ken could not see that his response was unbiblical and sinful. He would not accept how his response to conflict made the problem worse.

Ken is typical of many pastors drawn to the ministry to help people. They are merciful and often passive. Like many pastors who make counseling a primary focus of ministry, Ken needed to be needed. He loved the Lord and wanted to serve the church. But serving the church became his way to be accepted and loved. Slowly but surely the church was formed around Ken instead of the Lord Jesus Christ. Whenever a leader makes his need for support or empathy a core concern, the leader and church will fail.

Leaders prone to depression or to dramatic emotional highs and lows tend to be passive responders in conflict. At the low end of emotions, a leader's depression feeds upon the fear of rejection, increasing his loneliness and isolation, spinning down a cycle of despair. At the high end of emotions, the leader wants to paint all of life rose-colored. For some, a positivist, "word-faith" theology denies the reception or expression of any negative thought or word.

Spiritualizing Passive Behavior

Whether for positive or negative reasons, the passive response does not face the truth squarely. Passive responders, however, do not see themselves as deceptive. Focusing on their intense feelings and emotions, they believe that being passive is right, even Christlike.

It is not uncommon for leaders to spiritualize their passivity. We have worked with pastors who cite Isaiah, Matthew, and Peter as their proof texts:

> He was oppressed and afflicted, yet he did not open his mouth; he was led like a lamb to the slaughter, and as a sheep before her shearers is silent, so he did not open his mouth. (Isaiah 53:7)

> When he was accused by the chief priests and the elders, he gave no answer. Then Pilate asked him, "Don't you hear the testimony they are bringing against you?" But Jesus made no reply, not even to a single charge—to the great amazement of the governor. (Matthew 27:12–14)

> When they hurled their insults at him, he did not retaliate; when he suffered, he made no threats. Instead, he entrusted himself to him who judges justly. (1 Peter 2:23)

At the extreme, passive responders spiritualize their pain or conflict by portraying themselves as "suffering servants," innocent victims, or as being "crucified" unfairly like Jesus. As one pastor told me, "This board wants to crucify me."

While many boards are not supportive, and congregants can act more like a mob than a body, there is a great difference between an embattled pastor and the sinless Son of God. Vital distinction must be made, as we will see later, between Christ's refusal to defend or retaliate, and Scripture's exhortation to speak the truth in love.

LIKE TIMOTHY?

Timothy was probably passive. Scripture hints that Timothy was naturally timid and reluctant to confront. Yet the apostle Paul gave him some of the most challenging leadership assignments; the young leader assisted in Ephesus and Corinth. (See 1 Corinthians 16:8–11.) The evidence is that Timothy had his hands full. But Paul wrote to remind and exhort the young pastor to place his fears aside and allow God's Spirit to work in and through him. "For God did not give us a spirit of timidity, but a spirit of power, of love and of self-discipline" (2 Timothy 1:7; see also 2:14–15; 4:2).

Are you a Timothy? Are you prone to silence and other passive responses in conflict? Think about your Conflict Benchmark, measured at the end of chapter 4. As you review your thoughts, words, and actions—or in this case, silence and inactions—can you see where your response has contributed to the conflict?

WHAT YOU CAN DO TO CHANGE

If you recognize yourself in the preceding description, God wants you, like Timothy, to learn boldness. This starts with owning your weakness instead of celebrating it as a strength. A passive leader is not a leader.

You must change. It is likely that you will not change without a mentor who can lovingly but intentionally show you where and when and how you are being passive and give you suggestions about an alternative, redemptive response.

The goal is for you to be redemptive, not for you to be aggressive or defensive, which are equally counterproductive and harmful.

You will change as you submit to a process of learning how to be redemptive in your response to conflict. For you, this will mean learning skills of biblical confrontation and communication.

This might start with learning how to surface and say what you are thinking or feeling, even when you are not sure what it is or how to say it. For example, let's return to the boardroom scene that started this chapter. If you were in that room, what could you do or say to register your concern about Roger's aggressive proposal?

You might say, "As I've been listening to Roger's proposal, something feels wrong about it. I am not sure what it is exactly or even if I am right, but I need to explore this with you before I can vote on this."

This may generate a short or curt response from Roger, but it will also allow the group to ask you about what you are feeling and why.

A good exercise for a passive person is simply to think about and state an emotion that he or she is feeling with the reason. For example, "I am feeling (mad, sad, glad, frustrated, concerned) because . . ."

Back to the story above, you might say, "I am feeling concerned because Roger's proposal does not appear to address the . . ."

Your call and duty is to surface what God has placed on your heart or mind. You may not be the person to persuade others or defend your point of view, but you must speak.

Remember, your responsibility is to be a watchman. You goal is not to be loved or even right. Your call is to represent Jesus. Is the Holy Spirit bringing you a warning in your spirit? Perhaps you have discernment others do not have. You do not have to know this for certain. But you must speak.

A passive nature is the shadow side of a man or woman who has a heart for people because God has gifted him or her with mercy, hospitality, and other relational gifts, such as shepherding. God has given these gifts for the important role they play in God's redemptive purpose, a role that is stifled when a person is passive.

Being passive is ultimately cruel, unloving, and hurtful because it does not keep watch or warn against sin. "Better is open rebuke than hidden love. Wounds from a friend can be trusted, but an enemy multiplies kisses" (Proverbs 27:5–6).

EVASIVE RESPONDERS:
WHY YOU CAN'T
RUN OR HIDE

*But I said, "Should a man like me run away? Or
should one like me go into the temple to save his life? I
will not go!"*

~ NEHEMIAH 6:11

Is anything wrong?" Mary asked Greg in the hallway. Anxiety
immediately rose in Greg's mind as he stopped to talk. *She has some
nerve,* Greg said to himself, *asking me if anything is wrong.* All of the
hurt Greg felt from the last congregational meeting flooded through
his mind.

Two weeks earlier, Mary questioned a decision Pastor Greg made
in a staff meeting. He answered her question poorly, and when Mary
continued to press for the answer, he felt humiliated in front of the
group. He was mad at Mary for making him look unprepared and
foolish.

Greg was certain Mary was trying to make him look bad. In
fact, he was so convinced of this that he did not even bother to ask
Mary about it. Her question fit the pattern. Mary had not supported
him once in the two years since he became a leader.

To address this, loyalty was the subject of Greg's devotion in the next staff meeting. He did not give specifics or mention names, but he did say the staff needed to be supportive of one another. During the entire meeting he smiled easily and talked comfortably, but he never looked Mary in the eye.

Then at the board meeting last night, Greg suggested some staff changes might be needed in order to move ahead. When a board member asked if there were problems, the pastor answered, "No, we have a fine team. I just think we need some new people to sharpen us and give some new perspective." Then he observed, "You know, some of the staff have been here for years and years and it is hard for them to change, especially when a new leader comes in."

To illustrate, Greg mentioned that many churches have a policy that all staff resign whenever a new pastor begins. When a board member asked why he was bringing this up now, two years after coming, Pastor Greg backed away quickly. "This is not what I believe. It is just an illustration of how some churches handle change."

Mary was the only staff member with a long tenure. Some board members knew that the pastor and Mary had not seen eye to eye on several issues. But instead of addressing the issue directly to Mary or with the board, he used indirect communication.

The word quickly got to Mary that Pastor Greg wanted her to resign. That was the reason she stopped Greg in the hallway. And now the conversation begins.

"No, Mary, I'm fine," Greg answers. "I guess I'm a little tired. The board meeting went late last night." As he begins to step away, Mary reaches out her hand to stop him. "Are you sure there is nothing wrong between us? Isn't there something you need to talk to me about?"

Greg stops, smiles, and with all the control he can muster says, "No, really, Mary. I'm just tired. Everything is fine between us as far as I know."

Greg walks away congratulating himself that he kept his composure. *After all,* he rationalizes, *I never mentioned Mary's name in the board meeting.* At the same time, he grows more annoyed at Mary for stopping him in the hallway. *Once again, she is trying to embarrass me in front of others.*

In the following days the pastor talks to others about the need for everyone to support his leadership and the new church vision. He always has Mary in mind, but he is careful to be ambiguous and indirect. He suggests to Mary's best friend that if someone on the staff does not feel positive about where the church is going, perhaps he or she should think about looking elsewhere. When she asks if he has anyone in mind, Greg says, "No, of course not. I'd prefer everyone stay and work together. But if anyone cannot support where we are going, well, you know, it would be better for that person to recognize it."

This continues for several weeks, and soon the negative fallout begins. Though Pastor Greg wants Mary to resign, he never states that directly, hoping hints to friends and coworkers will do the job. Instead, the rest of the staff now wonders if he is doubting their performance or support. They begin to feel insecure and don't know who to trust, so they follow the pastor's lead by avoiding any confrontation and denying that any problem exists. Everyone feels that something is wrong, but no one is permitted to discuss it.

Meanwhile, Greg continues to tell Mary, "There's no problem here," hoping she will see the problem herself and decide to leave the church on her own. But Mary does not see the need to leave. Instead, she continues to ask hard questions about his leadership and direction.

FINALLY . . . VOICES OF CONCERN

Soon ministry momentum and progress slows. Members voice concern that goals are not being reached. An anonymous complaint comes to the governing board. A staff person confides that "things are very tense" in the church office. Then a prominent member voices a concern.

The board holds an emergency meeting to ask Pastor Greg what is wrong. At first he denies any problem; then he suggests that, perhaps, some disgruntled and disloyal staff might be spreading rumors. When asked for specifics, Greg mentions what Mary said in the staff meeting six months earlier. He says he does not know for sure, but that Mary may be undermining support. The board urges the pastor to confront Mary personally before the annual meeting, but Pastor Greg's schedule is busy, and he doesn't get around to making the call.

However, Greg does find time to confide in a few loyal members, letting them know the hurt he has felt and the pain he has been quietly enduring for months. They are shocked to hear that there is a movement afoot to "get rid of the pastor." These friends tell others, urging them to pray for the pastor, and to come give their support at the annual meeting.

THE EXPLOSION

At the annual meeting the conflict erupts into a shouting match. Months of pent-up anger and emotion are released on all sides. Pastor Greg is alarmed, disgusted, and very angry, but he says very little. The next day he resigns.

In the letter of resignation the pastor admits to some unspecified "mistakes in judgment" but adds, "I see now that it is best to leave peacefully rather than disrupt the church by challenging the 'handful' of people who feel they cannot support their pastor."

Privately, he tells friends that Mary "ran me out of the church."

This scenario, or one like it, is common for pastors and leaders who take a left-handed, evasive approach to handling conflict.

In fact, most pastors and most churches use evasive responses to conflict. They do so because they want everyone to get along and love one another. They choose to "keep peace" rather than make it.

DEFINITION AND DESCRIPTION OF EVASIVE RESPONDERS

To "evade," according to *Merriam Webster's Collegiate Dictionary,* is "to elude by dexterity or stratagem; to avoid facing up to; to avoid answering directly." Princeton University's WordNet defines *evasive* as being "deliberately vague or ambiguous; avoiding or escaping from difficulty or danger, especially enemy fire; and skillful at eluding capture."

If you are an evasive conflict responder, you will do almost anything to escape conflict or avoid "enemy fire." You will run away from sin and shirk responsibility for your mistakes. You will lie to yourself and others that you have been hurt when someone has sinned against you. You will divert an accusation or minimize the damage of your sin against someone else. You will avoid confrontation at all costs.

As you read the story above, you may have recognized yourself while denying that you actually do those things! This description cannot be you because it is too painful to see yourself this way. Perhaps you are evading.

People who use evasive responses tend to believe that all conflict is wrong and must be avoided. So evasive responders will almost always lie when questioned about a conflict. Ask evasive conflict responders, "Is something wrong?" and their first response will always be no. When forced to answer, they will divert the real issue to something of secondary or minor importance. And if the problem is still pursued, evasive responders will resort to spreading rumors, rationalizing their own behavior, or blaming others for the conflict, further compromising truth.

EVASIVE RESPONDERS AND TRUTH

Evasive responders are, by virtue of their response, deceptive. They are more interested in diverting themselves (and sometimes others) away from the discomfort and responsibility of the conflict than they are in reconciling themselves or others to God's truth.

Evasive responders will protect themselves by manipulating relationships to their advantage. Sometimes this will include twisting the facts to fit their arguments or circumstances. Evasive responders, unlike passive responders, will acknowledge that there is a problem but will go to great lengths to minimize or divert the problem.

On some occasions their evasion will simply be, "I don't want to talk about it right now." What they mean, of course, is that they never want to talk about it. On other occasions, evasive responders will attempt to convince themselves and others that the problem is not worth troubling over. Evasive responders are self-deceiving. However, they do not see themselves as dishonest. Instead, they see themselves as merciful and loving, protecting relationships.

EVASIVE RESPONDERS AND RELATIONSHIPS

Ironically, in their pursuit of preventing hurt, evasive responders will often deny or lose touch with their own feelings, preferring to accept the lie than to acknowledge the hurt. Some evasive responders have difficulty expressing love or affection and accepting it from or giving it to others.

While they say relationship is a supreme value, evasive responders tend to seek out only those relationships that support them and avoid or even sacrifice relationships that do not. Even close friends who honestly disagree with or seek to correct an evasive responder will be forfeited to avoid hurt.

When friends honestly and lovingly confront an evasive responder, they will often express frustration and confusion from the result. The friends leave the conversation feeling that their concerns were twisted, diverted, or turned back on them.

Evasive responders rarely experience genuine reconciliation because they are always minimizing, compromising, and settling for less.

TACTICS OF EVASIVE RESPONDERS

Evasive responders can be very persistent in changing or divert-ing the subject whenever a conflict surfaces. In fact, if they gave as much energy to reconciling the conflict as they did to avoiding it, they and the church would be far more productive and healthy.

Some evasive responders use humor. When a conflict or difficult issue is raised, they will divert the conversation by making a joke or using sarcasm. If they are challenged for this, they will say, "I was only kidding," or insist that you or others are too serious. When evasive responders are forced to face an issue, they will leave a meet-ing early or claim they "cannot talk about it right now."

Evasive responders can seriously sidetrack and confuse church boards and ministry teams. Just when a difficult issue is about to be addressed, the evasive responder will step in, raising questions or issues that frustrate and stall the progress.

Our ministry team has worked with several churches that had one person in leadership who was a wonderful person and sacrifi-cial servant, but whose presence in meetings constantly frustrated, confused, and delayed decision-making. Sometimes the person was the guy who personally built the church, who would mow the lawn every week, or who had painted the Sunday school wing four times in the past twenty-five years. Or the person was the dear lady who had never missed a service and faithfully played the organ every Sun-day for five decades, including the week her husband died five years ago.

No one wants to confront these dear saints, because they have done so much for the church. But they are evasive. If evasive respon-ders are not corrected, the church will stagnate, frustrating truly gifted leaders and prompting them, eventually, to leave the church.

Evasive responders frequently minimize problems in the church. To minimize means to negate or to reduce to a minimum the impor-tance of events, issues, and conflicts. In the church, evasive respon-ders will frequently make statements such as "Every church has problems," or "No church is perfect." They will insist that the problem is insignificant or common to every church.

In one church we served, the elders were evenly divided over competing ideas of vision and purpose. Some wanted the church to grow larger under a strong senior pastor. Others insisted that the church needed to grow deeper with the current associate staff, suggesting a senior pastor might not even be necessary. The church was stuck. Attendance plateaued, evangelism ceased, and corporate prayer waned. Leaders were directly responsible.

But when we met with the elders for a daylong retreat, several elders insisted that the church was actually in good health—the church was growing, evangelizing, and praying. They estimated "only a handful of people" saw leadership as a problem.

To test this, we recommended a churchwide assessment. It took the elders months to decide whether the church needed to be assessed. When they finally agreed, we interviewed 350 people and examined the records of the church.

In seven years the church had grown by about 2 percent, remaining relatively constant at 600 attendees. However, during the same time, the community the church served had grown by 100 percent. Had the church just kept pace with population growth, we would have expected to see attendance double or new churches planted.

In previous years the church had an effective Evangelism Explosion ministry. When this ministry stopped, nothing replaced it. When the elders called the church to a season of prayer, fifty people came. A month or two later, the prayer meeting had ten people coming regularly. And when we asked church members to complete the sentence "Our leadership is . . .", 95 percent of the responses were negative.

Minimizing diverts leaders and members from seeing, owning, and addressing the truth about a situation. Minimizing kills effective decision-making.

Ironically, if minimizing does not work, the evasive responder will often take the opposite approach, insisting that great harm will come if leaders address the subject directly or publicly. This is akin to a patient denying he has cancer until it is unavoidable, then claiming surgery and chemotherapy would hurt too much to help.

In the church, evasive responders are the first to protest public confession or church discipline, claiming that people will be hurt or leave the church, or that gossip will spread. Evasive responders do not understand that silence and evasion are the greatest cause of hurt and gossip.

Evasive responders are needy people. Their primary need is to be accepted, but always on their terms. Believing that any fault exposed will lead to rejection, evasive responders live in a world of constant denial. While most evasive responders are preoccupied with the negative, some evasive responders take the other extreme. These will spiritualize all potential conflict through a "word-faith" or "name-it, claim-it" kind of positive thinking, always attributing good intentions and innocence to all involved. In either case, the evasive responder will avoid any problem that may lead to rejection.

A COMMON KIND OF RESPONSE

Evasive responses are very prevalent in the evangelical church and can be seen clearest in one simple fact concerning church discipline. Most churches do not discipline their members because the member leaves long before the discipline process can be put in place. Confrontations typically go like this:

Pastor: "Fred, I understand you have left your wife."
Fred: "Yes."
Pastor: "You know what God's Word says about this . . . that you are called to love your wife."
Fred: "Yes, I know."
Pastor: "So, will you return to your wife and work on your marriage?"
Fred: "No."

Pastor: "Fred, if you will not return and be reconciled to your wife, you cannot sing in our choir, and we will take steps to discipline you."

Fred: "That's OK; I've decided to go to the church across town anyway. I can sing in their choir."

Leaders and congregants alike would rather leave the church than be reconciled.

EVASIVE RESPONSES IN OUR DENOMINATIONS

Evasive responses are common to denominations and institutions as well as individuals. A pastor sins. The regional leader of the denomination steps in to resolve the problem. Hearing all sides, he offers the pastor a deal. "If you go quietly, I'll help you find another church." The regional leader knows that this is not the best solution. But he also knows that a conflict in this single church will likely consume most of his time for the next six months if he doesn't find a way to resolve the problem quickly. Since he has one hundred other churches under him, he does not have the time, resources, or energy to confront every problem that comes up.

"Besides," the leader reasons, "this pastor is a good man. His entire ministry will be ruined if the word gets out." So the leader rationalizes his actions by minimizing the harm resulting from the pastor's sin.

If you think this does not happen, think again. This scenario plays itself out in many denominations.

A few years ago we conducted an assessment of a church where both the pastor and the regional leaders tended to be evasive in response to conflict. The pastor voted with his board for us to come and assess the church. A week before the date, he resigned and moved his family to another region.

I interviewed the pastor by telephone, asking him why he did not stay—telling him that the evidence indicated considerable unreconciled conflict. He responded by saying, "I know in my heart that I've done all I could already. I don't know how much more my wife and I can go through." When asked again, the former pastor said, "No. I will not do that." He went on to minimize both the conflict and the harm he caused, saying the problem between the church and him was simply "not the right fit."

In a confidential memo, we warned the pastor that our assessment found unfinished and unreconciled issues requiring further action. This included the need for members at Fourth Church to confess sin and ask forgiveness of the pastor, the need for the pastor to confess sin and ask forgiveness of members in the church, and the need for the pastor to explore privately, with mature Christian brothers, several negative issues in his life and ministry.

Further, we warned that if the patterns of thinking and behaving were not explored, reconciled, and corrected by the pastor now, they would likely be repeated in future ministry. Immediate entry into a new church pastorate could be hampered by the trauma and unfinished issues experienced at Fourth Church.

While the pastor ran away, the denomination looked the other way. The evasive response of each compounded the problem.

The pastor had moved out of the area. But he was going to serve a church in the same denomination. There was compelling evidence that the former pastor struggled with losing his temper, had a need to be in control, and had a degrading, even abusive, view of women. Should the pastor hurt someone in the future, the first questions asked would be, "Who knew there was a problem?" and, "What did they do about it?"

"We know this is difficult," we wrote to the denomination, "but the best way to handle these matters is to speak the truth in love." Our experience is that most denomination leaders do not want to face conflict, so they look for excuses not to, hoping the conflict will go away.

FEAR OF REJECTION

Evasive people have a pervasive fear of rejection. They want so much to be accepted and validated that any perception of rejection can lead to words and behavior that often, paradoxically, encourage acts of separation. Evasive Christians would rather leave than be rejected.

For instance, in a competitive game, evasive responders will quit before they lose. In work they will resign rather than endure correction. In church or marriage they will suddenly leave or run away rather than work out a conflict or disagreement. Often the evasive responder will overreact and take personally even the most general of concerns or criticisms.

In extreme situations, we have seen pastors sabotage their own ministry through intentional or willful sin. A pastor who is depressed or suffers through a prolonged period of doubt or failure will sometimes choose to sin in words or behavior that he knows will require his dismissal. He does so to control his own rejection and to gain a distorted sense of sympathy.

Evasive responders have a sympathetic, emotional view of grace and mercy. In conflict, they will constantly minimize sin and maximize the need for grace and mercy. Rather than have a sinner confess, receive forgiveness, and work out restitution, evasive responders simply want to "forgive and forget." Ultimately this is "cheap grace," what Dietrich Bonhoeffer calls "grace without the cross . . . justification of sin without justification of the sinner."[1]

LOSS OF TRUST

Trust, along with truth, is among the greatest casualties of evasive responses. Trust is based upon truth. Trust is broken when people sense their leaders are covering up or smoothing over sin. This is the great irony of evasive logic; in an effort to keep relationships and protect themselves, evasive responders do what endangers their relationships and reputations most: They avoid the truth and undermine trust.

There are times when it is appropriate for church leaders to say, "Trust us." There are few issues that the congregation needs to know every detail about. Leaders should have the congregation's trust to take care of the problems as leaders. But this requires open communication and a history of speaking truth in love. If the leaders are known to be evasive, smoothing over or avoiding problems in the past, trust will not be given. When this happens the church has two problems, not one: the presenting sin and the credibility of the leaders to address it.

Evasive leaders always fail because they lack the essential trust necessary for people to follow.

What You Can Do to Change

If you recognize yourself as an evasive responder, the gospel of Jesus Christ offers you the freedom and power to change.

If you struggle with issues of acceptance, identity, and esteem, the promise of Scripture is that God knew you and chose you before the creation of the world. He knows you by name. You are valuable and loved by your Creator. This love is demonstrated tangibly as well as emotionally. It is part of God's redeeming love that He allows rejection, weakness, and failure to enter your life so that you will look to Him alone for your strength.

God calls you to live and grow through your conflicts and failures, not to avoid them. In fact, your evasive response is keeping you from living into the calling you have received.

The power of sin or failure is what you make it. Every attempt to avoid or divert the pain is a step toward increasing its power over you. Worse, evasion denies the power of the Cross to forgive, redeem, and restore.

Your growth is being stunted because you are refusing to receive God's grace. This grace often comes through hurt, correction, and discipline.[2]

And you have forgotten that word of encouragement that addresses you as sons: "My son, do not make light of the Lord's discipline, and do not lose heart when he rebukes you . . . Endure hardship as discipline; God is treating you as sons. For what son is not disciplined by his father? If you are not disciplined (and everyone undergoes discipline), then you are illegitimate children and not true sons. Moreover, we have all had human fathers who disciplined us and we respected them for it. How much more should we submit to the Father of our spirits and live! . . . No discipline seems pleasant at the time, but painful. Later on, however, it produces a harvest of righteousness and peace for those who have been trained by it. (Hebrews 12:5,7–9, 11)

So, what can you do? First, confess your evasiveness to two or three brothers or sisters who can encourage you, support you, and hold you accountable. Second, ask God to reveal those events and issues in your life that you have evaded. Third, ask God to give you boldness and courage from Scripture, from His Spirit, and from others to face each of your conflicts directly.

Fourth, one by one, address each issue by calling the person or group involved to confess your evasiveness, ask forgiveness, and work out reconciliation. This will be extremely difficult at first. You will need the help and encouragement of friends. With time, however, you will develop new habits and confidence for leading.

Leadership and character are proved and refined in conflict. Conflict is an opportunity. God wants you to confess and renounce evasive patterns of thinking and behaving and to learn new habits of "speaking the truth in love."

Notes

1. See Dietrich Bonhoeffer, *The Cost of Discipleship* (New York: Macmillan, 1949), 45–47.
2. See also Psalm 94:12; Proverbs 1:7; 3:11; 6:23; 10:17; 12:1; 15:32; 2 Timothy 1:7.

Seven

DEFENSIVE RESPONDERS:
WHY YOUR CONFLICT
IS NOT ABOUT YOU

Why not rather be wronged? Why not rather be cheated?

~ 1 CORINTHIANS 6:7b

Eric would have made a great lawyer. His ability to communicate with passion, often without preparation or apparent forethought, was persuasive and powerful. But Eric was not a lawyer defending someone wrongly accused. He was a pastor defending himself.

We met Eric years ago when we were called in to assess his former church. He had resigned months earlier, but the congregation was still reeling from more than a decade of Eric's manipulative and defensive style of leadership. Toward the end of his ministry, Eric had grown increasingly defensive by promoting falsehood, claiming special status, and blaming others. His defensive words and behavior were heightened whenever Eric's position or power was questioned, or when money was the issue.

Yet Eric had remained popular with many in the congregation

who never threatened Eric and, consequently, never experienced his manipulation personally. (This popularity is often the case with gifted communicators.) So when Eric spoke of his suffering at the hands of troublemakers who were "out to get him," many believed him.

Eric knew how to manipulate people. The most disturbing of all the patterns was his use of spiritual authority for self-protection or personal gain. This was done in subtle and overt ways, such as:

- using Scripture to defend or protect himself
- comparing himself to the Messiah
- declaring special insight, knowledge, or revelation
- spiritual overstatement
- double-talk in preaching

Eric's letters and sermons often positioned him in "super-spiritual" terms, implying special revelation from God. Sometimes these messages were subtle and open for interpretation. Other times his "self-righteousness" served to promote himself and blame others.

For example, Eric wrote a letter to the elders late in his ministry stating, "I assume the position 'of a servant humbly sacrificing for the sake of Christ and his Church.' . . . 'I am fighting the fight. I have finished the course. There is laid up for me a crown of righteousness.' God has revealed that I will leave our church as a prophet and a 'suffering servant.'"

On at least two occasions, Eric used the Communion table to draw attention to himself in ways that were spiritually loaded and confusing. In each case, the suffering of Christ was compared to the pastor's condition. Eric would take the bread and say, "This is Christ's body, broken for you." Then Eric would speak of his personal pain and brokenness. Then he would mention the sacrifice of Christ and invite the congregation to eat.

The subject and focus moved from Christ to the pastor then back to Christ, equating the suffering of the pastor to that of Christ. The first and last part of each statement was biblical and true. The insertion of the pastor in the middle was a subtle and heretical form of saying "I am like Christ."

Eric's last sermon at the church was an archetype for virtually every dysfunctional pattern discovered in the course of our review. So many people spoke about the message that our ministry got a tape and listened.

The message was ambiguous and self-absorbed. Eric referred to himself so many times that we ended up counting every pronoun. He said "I, my, me, or myself" 366 times. He made reference to God, Jesus, or Spirit (including He, Him, etc.) just 109 times. The irony is that the theme of his message was "to let go" and allow God to work in your life. Nearly everything he said, and the manner in which he said it, denied the truth of this message in his own life.

Our assessment revealed Eric's repeated attempts to conceal information, twist facts, and overemphasize partial truths in order to blur the deeper issues. Over many years Eric repeatedly defended himself by:

- presenting partial, incomplete, or twisted truths
- using semantic and procedural roadblocks to squelch investigation
- concealing pertinent facts
- evading fundamental issues and core questions

These patterns were repeated time and again when the pastor's authority or power was challenged. When challenged directly about an issue, Eric would claim that the problem was merely a difference of "perception," "opinion," or "feelings."

He would not recognize the needs and hurts of others, but framed the conflict in terms of a debate over a difference of opinion or feeling. Then Eric would turn the argument against his accuser.

The problem was theirs because they were not "open" to varying viewpoints.

Our assessment heard numerous stories of members who went to discuss matters with the pastor personally, only to leave frustrated and confused. "We talked all around the issue," people told us, "but we never got to the core problem." Following the meeting the pastor would assume a posture of humility, suggesting that the problem was not with him but with the unwillingness of others to let go of their arguments or to forgive.

Eric often noted how he had followed the steps outlined in Matthew 18—going to or receiving privately the concern of a brother. However, the evidence revealed that Eric did not meet to be reconciled but to defend himself and turn the concern of the brother back against the brother.

Like many defensive pastors, Eric used the pulpit for his own therapy and self-justification. He preached on submission, gossip, and obeying authority after an event when his power was contested. By raising the specter of "gossip" continually, often with inflammatory rhetoric, Eric exacerbated rather than alleviated the problem.

Pastor Eric also controlled the flow of information. The governing board was frequently warned not to reveal anything discussed. (Such a rule is good but assumes a spiritual integrity in the decision-making process that is often not the case.) Members were frequently instructed "not to tell" something after meeting with the pastor. If a member questioned these and other issues, he would be labeled a "gossip."

Unity and gossip became constant themes in the pastor's reports to the congregation. Linking these two ideas was an interesting tactic. Unity came to be defined in political, not spiritual, terms. Unity meant agreeing or siding with the pastor. The subtle, sometimes overt, message was "If you disagree with the pastor you are against unity in the church."

CONTROL VERSUS OPENNESS

Board minutes demonstrated Eric's preoccupation, even paranoia, with secrecy and control. The pastor continually returned to reactive and adversarial themes of "how to stop gossip" or "how to stop disunity." The board took the bait, focusing on disciplining troublemakers. No one asked, "Why is gossip or disunity a constant problem in our church?" Or, "Is there something about the way we are governing that contributes to this problem?"

Openness to dialogue, speaking the truth in love, and seeking God's voice through dialogue and discernment were noticeably absent in the board and the congregation.

Our assessment heard from many in the church who met with the pastor about his leadership or manipulation. The stories were revealing by how similar they were, even though most people and events were unrelated. Members repeatedly told us the pastor would characterize the problem as a "misperception of what he said or did." In other words, he was not the problem. No attempt was made to understand or to resolve the dispute by uncovering truth. It was always a matter of "opinion" or "feelings," and "everyone is entitled to have their own opinion." People left the pastor unreconciled and frustrated. Afterward, these people became the object of the pastor's scorn.

In fact, we found no instance in which a leader or member of the church challenged the pastor's authority when that person did not resign his or her position, leave the church, or became the focus of an accusation shortly thereafter.

In six years, a total of twenty-three lay leaders and at least three staff members left their positions after protesting leadership at the church.

Every leader who challenged Eric became "a problem" to the church. Many of these leaders were initially supporters of the pastor. They became involved in leadership often at the request of the pastor. Significantly, whenever a problem appeared—or reappeared—

Pastor Eric responded to the confrontation by using defense and manipulation, which would force a choice between the pastor and those challenging him. The pastor always won.

In the final two years of Eric's ministry, approximately 250 people and over 116 families left the church. We sent out a reconciliation form to all 116 families and received 96 back, many with five or six typed pages telling us about their hurt.

When we met with Eric to discuss these findings, he claimed that he was the victim of a conspiracy.

We responded by saying, "Well, let's consider that option. On one side we have these letters and testimonies from hundreds of people—many of whom do not even know one another and most of whom represent totally different and unrelated issues. Yet, all describe your leadership as self-absorbed, manipulative, and defensive. Then we have waves of staff and elders who have come and gone during your ministry—two dozen or more people that *you* selected and then *you* said had to leave. All of these people left, yet the problem kept coming back. Why is that?

"Maybe you are right," we continued. "Perhaps all of these folks are part of some vast conspiracy against you. Or perhaps you are the problem. The only common denominator we have found is you."

Eric is an extreme example of a defensive responder. But perhaps you recognize some of his tactics. The following definition and description of defensive responders will help you see more of how destructive a defensive posture toward conflict can be—to you and to your church.

DEFINITION AND DESCRIPTION OF DEFENSIVE RESPONDERS

To be defensive is to protect or to justify oneself in the face of criticism, failure, or attack. Defensive responders are excessively concerned about guarding their position or reputation against real or perceived threats. They want to minimize exposure of their shortcomings.

People who use defensive responses tend to believe all conflict is about proving who is right and who is wrong, so authority and position must be defended at any cost.

People tend to use defensive responses when they are more interested in protecting themselves or their version of events than they are in finding God's truth or in restoring broken relationships. Defensive responders can be argumentative, persuasive, and manipulative. Defensive responders are outspoken in their opinions; they will often take extreme arguments to prove a point.

DEFENSIVE RESPONDERS AND TRUTH

To prove they are right, defensive responders will manipulate relationships and bend the truth in order to protect their position or reputation. Defensive people have a great need to be right. Their primary sin is that they would rather be right than reconciled.

Defensive responders will claim special knowledge, position, anointing or authority that makes them above correction. In some churches we have found pastors or spiritual leaders claim a special anointing, or a special status, based upon Scripture verses such as "Do not touch my anointed ones; do my prophets no harm" (Psalm 105:15). In interviews with members of Eric's church, several told us that they could never challenge the pastor because the pastor was God's anointed. "Where did you learn this?" we asked.

"Pastor told us," they said, often citing the verse in Psalms.

SCRIPTURAL TRUTH

This is a misuse and misinterpretation of Scripture. The command "do not touch my anointed" speaks to two situations. The first is David's refusing to raise his hand against the king of Israel—God's specially anointed king (1 Samuel 26:9). Being a pastor and the first king of Israel should not be equated.

The second situation, found in Psalm 105:15 (and elsewhere)

is a warning to pagans not to touch any Israelite. The "anointed ones" are Israelites—all believers. If this verse applies to the church, it is a warning to unbelievers not to touch any believer.

Spiritual anointing and authority is a Spirit-gift or grace, a divine empowerment. It cannot be earned, learned, or possessed. Scripture teaches all authority belongs to God; authority is given and taken away at His will. Man is merely a steward. When man uses divine authority for self gain, it is sin.

Spiritual anointing is about God, not man; not about experience, personality, talents, or even ordination. A gifting is not an innate "ability" but a divine enabling. A person is anointed when the Holy Spirit is operating through the person. There is no authority or anointing in a person or position apart from the Holy Spirit.

This is not to say that leaders or positions are unimportant. Scripture gives clear instructions to the church to honor leaders and to obey authority, with warnings against those who do not. However, with honor comes accountability. Thus Paul wrote:

> The elders who direct the affairs of the church well are worthy of double honor, especially those whose work is preaching and teaching. For the Scripture says, "Do not muzzle the ox while it is treading out the grain," and "The worker deserves his wages." Do not entertain an accusation against an elder unless it is brought by two or three witnesses. Those who sin are to be rebuked publicly, so that the others may take warning. I charge you, in the sight of God and Christ Jesus and the elect angels, to keep these instructions without partiality, and to do nothing out of favoritism. (1 Timothy 5:17–21)

Defensive responders will often claim or imply status over others by putting others down. My friend John Ryser calls this "status by negation." Status by negation simply means that "by putting you down, I elevate myself without ever changing." Jesus warned about such tactics after He told a parable "to some who were confident of their own righteousness and looked down on everybody else" (Luke

18:9). In the parable, two men, a Pharisee and a tax collector, entered the temple to pray.

> The Pharisee stood up and prayed about himself: "God, I thank you that I am not like other men—robbers, evildoers, adulterers—or even like this tax collector. I fast twice a week and give a tenth of all I get." But the tax collector stood at a distance. He would not even look up to heaven, but beat his breast and said, "God, have mercy on me, a sinner." I tell you that this man, rather than the other, went home justified before God. For everyone who exalts himself will be humbled, and he who humbles himself will be exalted. (18:11–14)

Jesus measures spiritual status by our ability to recognize and admit that we are sinners. Righteousness is a gift.

ARROGANCE AND POWER

Spiritual arrogance is common to defensive responders. Defensive responders will posture themselves by making bold and declarative statements concerning God's voice, using phrases such as: "God told me . . ." or "The Lord revealed to me . . ."

It is not a sin to claim you have heard from God. It is the sin of pride to present this untested, as a requirement for loyalty or spirituality.

Defensive people use power words and competitive language that encourage conflict. Doing so serves to frame the debate in such a way that any question or challenge to the defensive person is tantamount to challenging God. Few issues in life are so clear-cut.

Defensive leaders frequently have a "my way or the highway" approach to leadership. When confronted about an issue or with a disagreement about a decision, the defensive leader will often respond with a suggestion that "if you cannot support the direction of the church, perhaps God is leading you elsewhere." The tactic is always to place the focus on themselves and the blame on others. The test is always loyalty, often at the expense of truth.

As Eric's story above illustrates, defensive responders are quick to think the worst about others and to attribute hostile intentions or conspiracy to people who disagree. Once assumed, improvement is nearly impossible. Once you have crossed a defensive person, your relationship is likely to suffer dramatic change.

We served a church recently where thirty to forty people described their relationship with the pastor as "formerly best friends." In each case, the person confronted the pastor about sin in his life. In some cases, a decade of friendship was suddenly dropped. Defensive responders often have a conditional and skewed sense of loyalty.

Defensive responders often find spiritual excuses not to be honest. They will rationalize and defend their behavior or seek to puff themselves up by citing their achievements and sacrifices in the past.

We sat with one pastor who, when confronted by a brother in Christ, responded by saying, "John, how can you say that? You know, you would not even be a part of this church without me leading you to the Gospel ten years ago."

Citing facts or truths unrelated to the present issue is spiritual manipulation and has no place in reconciling conflict.

DEFENSIVE RESPONSES AND RELATIONSHIPS

Defensive responses are destructive because they prevent the sinner and the church from hearing and learning God's perspective. Even when a leader is wrongly accused, a defensive reaction is wrong.

Years ago, while serving as an intentional interim pastor, I learned that Susan in the church believed I "hated her." When I asked her about this, she said, "Pastor, three weeks ago I drove by the church parking lot and waved to you. You looked right at me and then turned your back. And I knew then that you didn't like me."

Many church conflicts start with issues no bigger than this. My first thought was selfish: *I don't have time for this.* But I caught myself and asked, "Susan, I honestly don't recall not waving to you. When did this happen?"

Susan mentioned the date when she was certain I had snubbed her. It happened to be a day when I was in another church halfway across the country. It could not have possibly been me. Susan had me confused with someone else.

Here, everything depended upon what I said next. I could easily say, "Look, Susan, I've got more important things to deal with than your petty concerns about people waving to you." I could tell Susan that she is loony or paranoid or a pain in the neck . . . or say, "Of course I care about you!"

Or I could see that Susan was hurt and that the problem was deeper.

Earlier in my life, I would have responded defensively. God led me to say this instead: "Susan, I am sure I was out of town that week. But there's got to be something more. I must be doing something that causes you to think that I hate you. That concerns me. Can we talk about it?"

Susan and I sat down to talk. I learned that I had been insensitive and unkind to Susan and to others. By my opening up to hear the truth, Susan showed me areas of my life God wanted to change. By being defensive, even when you're right, you miss the opportunity to learn and be reconciled.

Much of what we justify in our thoughts about others is simply spiritual arrogance.

BEWARE DECEIT

Defensive responders are quick to blame others for personal sin and failure. At times they may even bear false witness or make false accusations to excuse self and avoid responsibility.

Our ministry assisted a church several years ago where the wife of a church leader had sinned morally. When the sin became known to the leader, he immediately forgave his wife and began a process of tracking down every person who knew about the sin to require their silence. "You cannot tell anyone about this," the leader had said, "for the sake of the kingdom of God."

The leader was genuinely concerned about how his wife's sin would impact the church, especially new believers. Defensive leaders often claim to be protecting the church by their actions. In reality, they are protecting themselves and promoting self-interest. The kingdom of God needs no man-made protection, certainly not from the truth.

For several months the leader was able to keep the issue quiet, but when the sin eventually became known—as it always does—the leader found himself embroiled in two problems: his wife's sin and his deceit.

We spent five hours with the leader talking about how his cover-up and self-defense made the problem worse, not better, and undermined his trust with the congregation. The leader insisted that he had acted with grace and that the problem in the church was gossip. Satan was using this situation to undermine his authority and to divide the church.

In our work with conflicted churches, we find Satan gets blamed for many things more rightly belonging to human failure and sin. Satan was undoubtedly using the conflict in this church to confuse and to confound, but it was the leader's cover-up that gave "the devil a foothold."

Most defensive responders genuinely believe they are acting on behalf of the truth while their words and behavior promote deceit. Defensiveness delays reconciliation, giving Satan room to maneuver.[1]

SELF-PROTECTION AND SELF-PROMOTION

Defensive responders see their reputation or position as integral to God's plan. They worry out loud about those who seek to destroy the church through negative thinking or false accusations. Defensive people see their role as preserving the truth and guarding sound doctrine, failing to see how their defensiveness springs primarily from self-protection.

Defensive responders do not lie as much as they carefully select the facts that serve their interest. They will take a partial truth and drive it home.

A common defensive technique is to seek out "experts" who will take their side. We have had church pastors and elders give us pages of Bible commentaries, quotes from famous authors, or cite expert testimony that supports their point of view.

Wanting to strengthen their position, they demonstrate a greater need—that they would rather be right than reconciled. The apostle Paul asked the Corinthians, "Why not rather be wronged? Why not rather be cheated?" (1 Corinthians 6:7). Defensive responders reveal their heart when they pour all their energy into demonstrating why they are right and the other wrong. Why not be wrong and reconciled?

Years ago we served a church that had seen its congregation decline by 40 percent in ten years, due in great part to the failure of the senior pastor. The pastor was a good teacher, but he repeatedly failed to lead and to shepherd his flock.

When we met with the pastor to discuss these findings, he refused to admit his failure. Instead, the pastor used the following responses to defend himself and shift responsibility for his actions to others:

1. *Blame.* The pastor constantly stated that a major problem in the church was the congregation's "lack of commitment," even going so far as to tell the church, "You have made me what I have become." In one meeting, the pastor claimed, "I'd be a better shepherd if I had better sheep!"

2. *Hurt.* A constant claim of the pastor was that people had "hurt" him. The pastor saw himself as a victim, failing to distinguish how hurt can be both productive and redemptive. (Recall Proverbs 27:5–6.)

3. *Position.* The pastor insisted that "God called me" to the church
   and that "I will not leave until God tells me to."

These statements had some measure of truth. Some church
members did lack commitment. Some did treat the pastor unkindly.
We did not question the pastor's original call. What was troublesome
was the pastor's use of these responses to defend himself and to
excuse his own responsibility.

When a defensive leader is well-liked and a good communicator, it is hard to identify what the real problem is. Is the pastor being
manipulative or merely speaking truth? How do you discern the difference?

The answer is to follow the fruit. Scripture repeatedly exhorts
believers to test everything by spiritual fruit.[2] "By their fruit you will
recognize them" (Matthew 7:16).

A good question to ask in these situations is, "Who is the object
or subject of this concern?" Defensive responders continually make
themselves—their emotions, intellect, or spirituality—the object and
subject of concern. When this happens, something is amiss. All conflict must always be about our submission to the lordship of Christ.

Sometimes, defensive responders will use family members to
shield themselves, manipulate emotions, or to engender sympathy.
We worked with one pastor who refused to be confronted by his
elders without his wife and two teenage girls present. His wife would
react in anger, and his daughters would promptly cry when their
father was "attacked." Later, the pastor pointed to how cruel the
elders were to his family.

Once, our ministry heard from the pastor of a church that we
had served two and a half years earlier. The pastor sent us a letter
claiming, among other things, that we had upset his marriage and
were responsible for the waywardness of his teenage son. His wife
and son, the pastor claimed, were distraught over our assessment.
Many members of the church had given testimony that the pastor
was a defensive and controlling leader. We reported this and sug-

gested that the pastor take a sabbatical to address these flaws. The pastor refused to accept or to act upon the assessment. That was the end of our involvement.

A leader's response to criticism will prove or disprove the validity of the criticism. In this example, the pastor was using his family to defend himself in order to prove he was not defensive. Always follow the fruit.

WHAT YOU CAN DO TO CHANGE

The problem with defensiveness is that efforts to justify or to promote self are usually seen by everyone except the defensive person. It might be hard for you to see yourself truthfully. You will need the honest input of others to change.

God wants you to change. Change starts with recognizing how your first impulse to defend always makes the conflict worse. Conflict is always about bringing our differences and concerns under the lordship of Jesus Christ. Lordship is always the key issue for leadership.

When Samuel became old and made his sons judges over Israel, the elders of the nation came to Samuel to demand a king. Samuel prayed to the Lord, who, in effect, said, "Look, Samuel, this is not about you." God said: "It is not you they have rejected, but they have rejected me as their king" (1 Samuel 8:7). As always, it is a matter of lordship.

When a leader is defensive, the debate pivots from God to man. Focus is given to the leader's power, position, or persuasion, not to God's voice or will.

Being defensive is actually self-defeating because it welcomes people into a critical evaluation of you—what you said or did or did not say or do. Now the energy of the church is to prosecute you. You, in turn, are encouraged to hide your faults, cover facts, and emphasize partial truths that support your cause. Being defensive breeds defensiveness.

The remedy for this is to simply stop defending yourself. Submit to God and to others. Ask God to reveal the truth in your life and others.

There is great freedom in allowing God to be Lord. Seek His counsel in prayer and accept *His* leadership; submit to Him in humility.

If you are a defensive responder, some of the most freeing words you can say are these: "I don't know. I believe. Will you walk with me in faith?"

But what should you do if you are accused falsely?

We frequently receive E-mails and letters saying we are being used by Satan. Even after ten years, those letters are not easy to read, nor are they taken lightly. But we read them because God may have something for us to hear or learn. That was not always our attitude. Early in the ministry we wanted to rebut and defend.

Then one day a friend gave me the book *A Tale of Three Kings* (Tyndale), by Gene Edwards. This short but powerful little study in biblical brokenness and submission follows the life of King David in his dealings with Saul and Absalom. David never defended himself. He always left vindication and justice to God.

The writer of Second Samuel told a humorous story that illustrates David's humility. As King David approached a city, a man named Shimei greeted the king with curses, pelting David and his officials with stones and yelling, "Get out, get out, . . . you scoundrel!" This irritated one of David's warriors. "Why should this dead dog curse my lord the king?" he said to David. "Let me go over and cut off his head" (2 Samuel 16:6–7, 9).

But David responded, saying,

> "Leave him alone; let him curse, for the Lord has told him to. It may be that the Lord will see my distress and repay me with good for the cursing I am receiving today." So David and his men continued along the road while Shimei was going along the hillside opposite him, cursing . . . and throwing stones at him and showering him with dirt. (16:11–13)

You may have a Shimei in your church. If so, what is your response? God may be using the sin of others to teach you something about yourself and Himself. Are you willing to learn? Or do you have more standing than David to insist on defending yourself?

Vindication and justice always belong to God, never to man. (More on the vindictive response and its dangers in the next chapter.) David knew and practiced this. When David had every opportunity and reason to kill Saul, who was pursuing him, David did not. Instead, he told Saul, "May the Lord be our judge and decide between us. May he consider my cause and uphold it; may he vindicate me by delivering me from your hand" (1 Samuel 24:15). Throughout the psalms, David brought his case before the Lord. He lamented over his suffering and called upon God for vindication.[3]

This is not to say that a leader should never respond to criticism or explain a decision. We are always called to speak the truth in love. But a leader should never defend. If correction, rebuke, or discipline is necessary against a false accusation or dissension, it is the work and role of fellow leaders (elders or deacons) to respond, not the one accused. Here is one more reason why churches should be led by an interdependent, collaborative team, not one person.

Never let power or position be the issue. Always make the lordship of Christ the issue. God can use you, like David, if you are willing to be broken. The following exercise may help your thinking.

AN EXERCISE

Here is an exercise to help you develop a humble heart and effective leadership style. Read through the biblical account of David in 1 Samuel 8 through 2 Samuel 23:8. Then read Gene Edwards's short novel, *A Tale of Three Kings*. Earmark quotes that might apply to your situation or conflict.

After you have finished the reading, ask yourself the following questions:

1. What does it mean to be broken?

2. What does true brokenness look like? Describe what David did and did not do as a model of brokenness.

3. Edwards's book describes the leadership style of three kings: Saul, David, and Absalom. (Though never recognized by God as king, Absalom proclaimed himself king and had a group of loyal followers; for a while he usurped David's position [2 Samuel 15:7–14].) Summarize each style. Which king have you (personally) and the leadership (collectively) been most like?

4. What passages of Scripture or quotes from the book stood out as speaking to issues you must face?

5. How have you fostered submission?

6. How have you fostered rebellion?

7. What has God revealed through this study that you must confess, confront in others, and reconcile to make restitution in the body?

8. What, specifically, will you do? When? How?

Notes

1. See Ephesians 4:25b–27.
2. Also see Psalm 92:12; Isaiah 5:4; Jeremiah 2:21; Matthew 3:10; 7:16–20; 12:33; Luke 3:8–9; 6:43–44.
3. See, for example, Psalms 26:1; 35:24; 43:1; 54:1.

AGGRESSIVE RESPONDERS:
LEAVING VINDICATION
FOR GOD

*Do not repay anyone evil for evil. Be careful to do what is
right in the eyes of everybody. If it is possible, as far as it
depends on you, live at peace with everyone. Do not take
revenge, my friends, but leave room for God's wrath, for it is
written: "It is mine to avenge; I will repay," says the Lord. . . .
Do not be overcome by evil, but overcome evil with good.*

⟿ ROMANS 12:17–19, 21

Jack always got what he wanted. Growing up in a strict, authoritarian home under an influential father, Jack learned early that survival went to the fittest and the strongest. "A winner never quits," Jack was taught. Problems were to be faced head-on, matched strength for strength.

Jack felt God's call to ministry as a young man. He grew up determined to be a soldier for Christ. Jack had that unique combination of drive and talent. He was a good student, natural athlete, and gifted communicator.

Jack was also a very angry young man. When his anger was channeled to sports, Jack excelled. He was the kind of star player coaches love and fear. When things got tough, Jack grew intense. You could count on Jack to provide the sheer determination and brute strength to win and to punish the opposition. But you never knew when Jack was going to explode.

Jack pastored as he played hockey. His muscular physique and short emotional fuse attracted and intimidated all around him. If you crossed Jack, you were going to pay for it.

From the first day he came to Fifth Church, Jack made it clear that he was the boss. Fifth Church had been a traditional church. Jack believed in a "seeker" approach. In Jack's first week as pastor he had the pews ripped out, the pulpit removed, and the cross at the front of the church taken down. When long-time members came to church the following Sunday, they were offended and shocked. When members expressed their concern, Jack grew intense and impatient. "I told you my philosophy of ministry before I came. If you did not want this you should not have hired me."

The first of three church splits occurred that first year. Half of the 300 members left. By the end of his tenth year, the church had grown to 700, but an equal number of people had also left the church, most unreconciled.

With each conflict, Jack responded with the same "my way or the highway" approach. "This is the way it is," Jack would say. "If you don't like it you can leave." When members and staff approached Jack about his anger and forceful style, Jack would explain, "That's the way I am. I'm not going to change. If a man does not understand strength, it's his problem, not mine."

Jack changed the church from congregational to elder rule. Then Jack surrounded himself with people loyal to him. He appointed the governing board and hired the staff.

Jack was a star player, not a captain or coach. He did not know how to mentor people or how to build a team. All the energy in the church was given to keeping Jack happy. When Jack was not happy, he threatened to resign. If a decision was not going his way he would tell his staff or board, "If we don't go ahead with this, then I will leave." Jack threatened to resign at least once a year for a decade. It always worked. The board and staff always backed down. Jack always got his way.

Through the years Jack often talked about his anger, even mentioned it from the pulpit. He would tell stories about "losing his cool" or saying things he should not. Many in the church saw this as being "authentic."

Fifth Church prided itself as a place where people could "come as you are." People did come. Jack had a passion for people who were hurting. He would do anything for someone down and out. The people Jack helped loved him as much as they needed him. They came in droves to hear him preach. Many people came to saving faith in Christ. But few grew beyond their struggles. In ten years, Fifth Church became a dysfunctional and divided church, a mirror image of its angry and aggressive pastor.

Jack is one example of a right-handed leader who responds aggressively to conflict. Perhaps some of his behavior is familiar to you or a leader in your church.

Aggressive responders tend to be very capable and likable leaders who attract a loyal following. They accomplish much. But the "shadow" side of their gifting can wound people deeply and ultimately destroy a church. The following descriptions will help you understand how aggressive responders think and act, and why God would have them change.

DEFINITION AND DESCRIPTION OF AGGRESSIVE RESPONDERS

To be aggressive means to be eager to fight; to initiate confrontation; attack, argue, or use emotional, spiritual, and physical force to defeat opposition. An aggressive conflict responder is hostile to any hint of criticism or disagreement.

People who use aggressive responses tend to believe all conflict is about power, so they view conflict as an opportunity to see who is the strongest or who is in control. Aggressive responders are more interested in protecting self and forcing truth than in preserving a relationship. They are competitive, forceful, pushy, vigorous, and energetic in conflict. Aggressive responders are confrontational. They are bold and assertive in their feelings. They are "Type A" personalities—highly motivated and gifted people who are dominant, direct, and demanding.

The primary need of an aggressive responder is to be in control. Aggressive responders tend to think and act in terms of power. This power may be physical, verbal, or intellectual but is always hierarchical and confrontational. For this reason, aggressive leaders are more frequently found in more conservative Independent, Fundamentalist, and Pentecostal churches.

Aggressive responders can be extremely focused and narrow in perspective, unwilling to compromise. They draw clear lines of right and wrong, good and bad. If you are not with them, you are against them. There is seldom a middle ground.

Aggressive people tend not to be aware, or even have sympathy, for those they have hurt. Hurting people is the inevitable and necessary "collateral damage" of spiritual warfare.

Most aggressive responders are excited by competition and frequently use analogies of warfare and sports to illustrate their decisions or sermons. Aggressive people will make even the simplest of tasks about winning and losing.

AGGRESSIVE RESPONDERS AND RELATIONSHIPS

In the church, aggressive responders are usually sincere and dedicated people who have a passion for the church but have never been personally broken. When a conflict surfaces, the aggressive responder will reflexively want to control. Since authority and position is all-important, aggressive responders are willing to sacrifice relationships and force what they understand to be the truth in order to protect or promote their position.

This right-handed approach to conflict is unbalanced because it emphasizes truth over love. It is about power, not relationship.

Aggressive responders are easily threatened and very sensitive to any form of criticism or disagreement. To prevent these, aggressive people will use force to intimidate or to attack. This force can be verbal or physical.

Verbally, aggressive people can be hurtful and demeaning in conversation, often celebrating these traits as a sign of their truthfulness. They will even use physical violence or threaten to damage a person financially or professionally. Typically the physical outburst will occur outside the church (though not always), and members will hear about it.

We know one pastor who was dismissed after repeated angry, physical outbursts both outside and within the church, which included a vulgar shouting match and object-throwing confrontation in the church office.

Aggressive responders believe the best defense is a good offense. If they can attack and keep the focus on others, they will not have to own or address their own failures. So aggressive responders will seek to gain influence over others through shame or excessive guilt. Shame is humiliating disgrace. It is a powerful and damaging emotion that should never be forced upon anyone. Aggressive leaders will use shame to humiliate fellow leaders in staff meetings or members in church services. They will use public forums to discuss private concerns. They do so to manipulate and to control.

Many aggressive leaders are intensely focused upon and committed to Scripture. Aggressive leaders are structured and orderly. They see Scripture as God's standard or guidebook for living. This leads many aggressive leaders into legalism. Their zeal for truth belies their lack of love and grace.

LAWSUITS AND A DESIRE TO WIN

When attacking and shaming fail, some aggressive responders will use the threat of legal action to get their way. Lawsuits are more and more common in churches.

Recently we worked with a church whose youth pastor had a homosexual encounter with a minor while on a youth retreat. When this was brought to the attention of the pastor and he was confronted, the youth pastor sued the church. Lawyers immediately stepped in and prohibited any contact between the parties for dialogue or reconciliation. Ultimately, the suit was thrown out of court but not until after a year of legal wrangling, financial cost, and spiritual upheaval.

Aggressive responders want to win. They seek to defeat anyone who disagrees with or threatens their power or position. For aggressive responders, winning means more than coming out ahead. It means defeating and punishing the opponent.

Aggressive leaders want to vindicate themselves and justify their actions. We believe the reason most leaders are never vindicated when wronged is that the leader would be the focus of glory, not God. Aggressive responders typically have an inflated sense of self-importance that often masks deep-seated feelings of inadequacy. Power hides the fear. Aggressive people can speak about themselves humbly while acting with great arrogance.

THE THREAT OF RESIGNATION

Paradoxically, most aggressive leaders are at once extremely fearful *and* overwhelmingly confident about how their church would survive without them. Aggressive people believe that the church would not make it without their involvement. Frequently, aggressive leaders will test this by using resignation as a weapon. At the same time, if anyone "calls their bluff" by accepting the resignation, the aggressive responder will immediately withdraw the offer and attack.

A good rule of thumb all leaders should use whenever a person threatens to resign is this: Immediately say, "I accept." Do not allow the leader to withdraw the resignation. If a leader uses resignation as a play for power or sympathy, you do not want that person leading your church. Period. Resignation must never be used or considered for any reason other than a genuine desire to seek or follow God's prompting. Always accept a resignation when offered.

We served a church that was in severe financial crisis due to the debt of a building project. Years earlier, the church board was warned about building prior to securing the funds or pledges for support. When people recommended that the church delay the construction project until funds were raised, the senior pastor gave an ultimatum: "Build now or I resign." The church built the building. Six months after the new facility was opened, the pastor left, and the church was stuck with a multimillion-dollar debt.

In another church, the pastor used the same technique for a different purpose. The pastor continually played the victim in order to get sympathy. Since the pastor was well-liked by his congregation, the board was afraid of an abrupt resignation. Whenever a problem arose, the pastor threatened to resign. Discussion stopped and the issue was diverted. This went on for years. When the elder board asked us what they should do when the pastor threatened to resign, the answer was short and simple, "Accept."

Church leaders can never allow a threat of resignation to sabotage decision-making or manipulate the church. This damages the church and reveals a critical character flaw in the leader. Any leader who uses a threat of resignation for sympathy or for power should not be in leadership. The church should accept the resignation immediately. If you don't do this, the problem will grow worse. In fact, in every church we have served where a leader threatened to resign, the church ended up firing or forcing the leader to resign later. In each church, the emotional and spiritual turmoil was made worse by not accepting the first resignation.

WHAT YOU CAN DO TO CHANGE

If you see evidence of aggression in your response, seek out a group of men (if a man) or women (if a woman) who will hold you accountable and will meet and pray with you regularly. Learning to own your feelings by regularly gathering with others to confess sin and to articulate your emotions will at first be difficult but ultimately very productive. Become comfortable with stating the reason for your feelings. "I feel angry because . . ."

Unlike passive and evasive responders, however, who must learn what more to do or say, aggressive leaders must learn how to bridle their words and actions. Like defensive responders, aggressive leaders will benefit from a study in brokenness and humility. (See the exercise that concluded chapter 7.)

More important and fundamental, if you recognize yourself as an aggressive responder, let God change your thoughts and habits about leadership.

First, you need to be freed from the false and secular thinking that leadership is about power or position. All of your notions about defending truth, protecting authority, and guarding sound doctrine boil down to either the sovereignty of God or your pride.

The startling and humbling fact is that God's truth and His church need you for nothing. There is nothing you can offer that can somehow complete His sovereignty or will.

Ultimately, all conflict is about lordship. The only question is, "Who will be lord of your conflict? You, or God?"

Shortly after Simon Peter was praised for recognizing Jesus as "the Son of the living God," he was rebuked for assuming this guaranteed an earthly kingdom established by right-handed power. Christ's kingdom and exaltation comes, instead, through humility and suffering.[1] Leadership is servanthood. It is washing your betrayer's feet. Note Jesus' example in John 13:4–17. Are you greater than Christ that you might refuse to wash your brother's feet? Can you respond to conflict as a servant of the King?

This is a mind-set, a way of life, that considers others before yourself—especially in conflict.

Second, God would have you learn how to lead in truth, not power. The godly leader never confronts power with power, but always confronts power with truth, and always in love.

Jesus said, "Do not resist an evil person. If someone strikes you on the right cheek, turn to him the other also" (Matthew 5:39). Turning the other cheek means taking two hits. If someone strikes you once, Jesus said, let him strike you again *without responding*. We think that if we turn the other cheek, the person will not strike again. They will. And when they hit twice, we feel we have grounds to respond. We don't.

Everything depends upon what you do with the second hit. If you hit back, you will launch a fight. But if you take two hits without retaliation, the third hit will not come. That's why Jesus said, "Turn the other cheek." It takes two to fight, and two hits to demonstrate that you will not respond in kind. This is the way of the Cross.

Since aggressive leaders frequently struggle to manage their anger, holding their tongue and resisting retaliation are habits that are nearly impossible to learn alone. You will be helped most by surrounding yourself with strong, loving people whom you give permission to speak into your life. Ask them to help you find healthy and non-competitive ways to express your intensity, anger, or frustration in productive ways, such as through music, writing, art, or physical exercise.

Third, you must ask God to help you make the lordship of Jesus Christ—not your position, power, or control—the issue. David Hansen has described the difference between a leader's becoming a parable versus a symbol.[2] Most leaders want to be symbols. God calls us to be parables.

The cross of Jesus Christ is a symbol. You look at the cross, and you see Jesus Christ crucified. You remember the cost of salvation: His grace, not our works. Jesus' life, death, and resurrection are the focus. A symbol is permanent. The cross reminds us of our hope in Christ.

A parable, on the other hand, is temporary. It serves as a picture that quickly goes away. Jesus told His disciples, "The kingdom of heaven is like a mustard seed; it starts out very small, but grows very large" (Matthew 13:31–32). The mustard seed gives a picture. Once the picture is understood, the seed is unimportant. The subject is the kingdom, not the seed. A parable is a picture that points to a subject, then gets out of the way.

Leaders are called to be parables, not symbols, to always make God the subject, not self. It is to say with John the Baptist, "He must become greater; I must become less" (John 3:30).

That is the art of spiritual leadership: to make Jesus Christ the object and the subject of everything you do. Never make the conflict about you. Make the conflict about submission to the lordship of Jesus Christ. Point to Jesus and get out of the way.

Notes

1. Isaiah 53:2–12; Philippians 2:5–11.
2. David Hansen, *The Art of Pastoring: Ministry Without All the Answers* (Downers Grove, Ill.: InterVarsity, 1994), 130–32.

Nine

CHURCH CONFLICT AND COUNTERFEIT PEACE

*Those whom I love I rebuke and discipline. So be
earnest, and repent. Here I am! I stand at the door and
knock. If anyone hears my voice and opens the door, I
will come in and eat with him, and he with me.*

∽ REVELATION 3:19–20

In the previous four chapters we discovered four common
responses to conflict. All are negative. All will lead the responder
and the church into greater harm and deeper conflict.

We learned that people who emphasize a "left-handed" approach
to ministry emphasize love and mercy at the expense of truth, frequently employing passive and evasive conflict responses. In contrast,
people who take a "right-handed" approach to ministry, emphasizing
truth and law at the expense of love, tend to employ defensive and
aggressive conflict response styles.

Each style is negative because it falls short of biblical peacemaking principles. Each style will lead to frustration and failure
because it is ultimately self-centered—based upon self-protection or
self-promotion. Each exchanges biblical truth and love for self-truth
and self-love. Each denies the power of the Cross and the lordship

of Jesus Christ.

Recognizing and owning your negative response style is the first step to understanding your part in a conflict and how your response may actually be making the conflict worse. Our purpose is not to have aggressive people be more passive, nor encourage evasive people to be more defensive. All the above styles are sinful. God calls His people and His church to be redemptive—not passive, evasive, defensive, or aggressive.

EVASIVE CHURCHES

You may have seen yourself and your church in one or more of the negative responses. Your conflict style is the arena where you will tend to sin most often—against God, others, and yourself. Every person sins. Every person has a negative conflict style that has been learned and practiced over time. This may be personality or culture driven.

In their collective response to conflict, most churches we serve are functionally evasive to conflict. Evasive thinking and acting breeds evasive communication. This is often the source of gossip and what we call *triangulation*. Rather than address issues in a personal and straightforward manner, church members use indirect, sinful communication.

THE SIN OF TRIANGULATION

Each spring for several years, I helped lead a mentoring workshop at a theological seminary on the East Coast. More than forty interns came for a three-day training in advance of their six- to twelve-month internship. They were paired with local pastors for the seminary mini-course. My topic was always conflict and communication.

I often spoke about triangulation, predicting the following to the interns: "Sometime in the first three weeks of your internship, you will be visited by a person in the congregation who wants to talk with you about the pastor, an elder, or some leader in the church. He may be a leader himself and will likely preface his remarks with kind words and good intentions. Do not be fooled. He is a minister of doom. If you listen, you will be party to death by triangulation." This got their attention and introduced a simple but vital teaching that every church leader and member must take to heart.

The word *triangulation* is taken from the field of trigonometry, referring to a method of surveying a region by dividing it into triangles. An unknown point can be determined by measuring distances between two known points. Relational triangulation occurs when a believer who has a problem with another believer talks to a third party (a friend, a wife, a coworker) about the problem before talking to the person in question. This is called triangulation because it brings a third party into a matter between two. Triangulation is always sin.

Matthew 18:15 clearly states that when a brother has knowledge of an offense against another, he is to go to that person quickly and directly. It is never right to talk to another person about a brother or sister without talking to the brother or sister first. Triangulation is a sin against the other person, the church, and the third party because it serves to separate, not unite; it breaks oneness and violates a trust.

The body of Christ is called to embody forgiveness—the outworking of our oneness in Christ. Our life together is founded upon the Cross—the power of forgiveness, which we work out in community.

Triangulation is an affront to the Cross because it robs a fellow believer of the opportunity for understanding, forgiveness, and reconciliation. If I go to a friend to talk about you instead of going to you, I have sinned against you in two ways. First, I have kept you from knowing there is a problem and robbed you of the opportunity to ask forgiveness. Second, I have sinned against you by talking about you behind your back.

Triangulation always makes the problem worse than it actually is. It is bad enough that I have talked about you to one other person, but once started, triangulation rarely stops. It is likely the person I talk to will talk to someone else who, in turn, will talk to others. Before long the entire church is talking about a problem that could have, and often would have been settled quietly between the two of us.

Triangulation can kill a church. We have seen it destroy many pastors and leaders—both victims and perpetrators. In some churches we have served, we can "map" or "survey" the church conflict by following the communication triangles.

Yet we frequently find leaders and members who have convinced themselves that their "special circumstances" make them exempt from following Matthew 18:15.

EXCUSING TRIANGULATION

Below are excuses commonly given for the sin of triangulation—talking to others instead of to one's brother first. You will note how each springs from the negative conflict response styles discussed above.

- *Legalism.* The matter was not a sin, "so technically, Matthew 18:15 does not apply." Defensive responders frequently will use technical logic like this to explain disobedience. In fact, the matter does become sin as soon as you talk about your brother behind his back.

- *Minimizing.* Evasive responders will rationalize triangulation by claiming the matter was too small to bother confronting. "I thought it would go away." If the matter is not worth confronting, then it should be overlooked and forgotten, never discussed with others or brought up later. Instead, most people keep a record of small things that pile up into a big thing that is later dumped on someone unsuspecting. The classic and common example of this is the elder board that meets in secret session, while the pastor is on vacation, to vote for his dismissal. They assume he knows the problem because the evidence is "overwhelming," yet often the small issues were never seriously addressed with the pastor in person.

~ *Blaming.* Defensive and evasive responders will use sympathy and blame to excuse triangulation. "No one can ever talk to Joe. He won't listen. . . . Poor Mrs. Smith would be intimidated, threatened or hurt going to him alone. . . . No one should confront Joe alone." Matthew 18:15 does not say, "Go, unless the brother is hard to deal with." It says, "Go."

~ *Displaying a false humility.* Passive and evasive responders will claim innocence or humility to excuse their triangulation, saying, "I thought maybe I was the problem. I talked with my wife and a few close friends to see what they thought. They convinced me that I was right because they felt this way too!" The best way to test your feelings is to talk with the person directly.

~ *Displaying a false compassion.* Passive and evasive responders will express compassion that is less than loving. "I did not want to hurt or judge." Often our efforts to protect people from hurt end up bringing more pain. This reason is frequently used for not confronting people who have emotional or psychological problems—as if the Cross had no power over depression, etc. We are our "brother's keeper." If we cannot give and receive truth in love, especially when it hurts, we are not participating in the body of Christ.

Here, as elsewhere, we take the simple but increasingly uncommon view that God knows better. If Christians will simply obey, that is, do what Scripture says, God is faithful to work all things together for good.

STOPPING TRIANGULATION

When someone comes to you to talk about a problem he or she is having with another person, your response should take the following four steps:

1. Stop and inquire. Before the person can tell you the problem, stop him or her immediately, then ask, "Have you talked to the person yet, and if so, when and where?" Many times people will say, "I tried." Ask them, "How did you try?" and "When did you try talking?" It is likely that they didn't really try; they knew they should go but were afraid. Some will say, "I called on the phone, but it was busy. I left a message, and they never called me back."

2. Warn. You might say, "Please don't talk to me about anything concerning another person until you've talked to the person about your concerns first." Warn the person that he is "triangulating"—bringing a third party into a matter that is really between two—and that triangulation is a sin against the person they are speaking about.

3. Affirm. Encourage the person to go talk to the person with whom he has conflict as soon as possible, affirming to the person that God will work in that situation as he obeys Matthew 18:15. Explain that "God will honor your desire to go and make things right."

4. Hold accountable. Then tell the person you will check back with him later to hear how the confrontation went. "In fact, it is so important for you and the other person to talk this out that I'm going to ask you next week how it went."

Triangulation and each of the four negative conflict responses above are flawed because they are based upon counterfeit assumptions and conclusions about peace. Before we move on to discover how to respond redemptively to conflict, we will examine the difference between true and counterfeit peace.

TRUE AND COUNTERFEIT PEACE

The Hebrew word for peace is *shalom*. Shalom is not a feeling of peace; it is a covenant of peace. It is complete, encompassing the whole of life. This is not possible to achieve on one's own. *Shalom* implies a relationship with God and others. Biblical peace is incarnational; it's the gift, evidence, and fruit of Christ reconciling the world to Himself. As Jesus said, "Peace I leave with you; my peace I give you. I do not give to you as the world gives" (John 14:27).

Christ's peace is different in nature and form from the world's peace. Christ's peace is costly because it required the Cross. This peace reconciles and restores completely. It is a gift that cannot be earned. The world cannot offer reconciling peace.

The world's peace is manmade, so it lacks spiritual fruit: love, joy, patience, kindness, goodness, faithfulness, gentleness and self-control (Galatians 5:22). The world can only offer law or cheap grace. Either way, it's merely temporary relief or compromise. As God Almighty warned, "They dress the wound of my people as though it were not serious. 'Peace, peace,' they say, when there is no peace" (Jeremiah 6:14).

FIVE KINDS OF FALSE PEACE

There are at least five ways the world gives peace. Each falls far short of Jesus' reconciling peace, yet we find all five commonly practiced in the church. We might label these practices: (1) personal peace, (2) agreeing to disagree, (3) forgiving and forgetting, (4) peacekeeping, and (5) détente.

1. PERSONAL PEACE

When Christians make statements such as "I am at peace with the situation," they are claiming a kind of "personal peace." Personal peace is understood as a state of inner contentment or serenity: a peace of mind.

Christians often use personal peace to avoid confession or confrontation, claiming, "I am at peace," therefore reconciliation is not necessary. Personal peace is spiritually bankrupt because it turns biblical peace into a possession, an emotion, and, ultimately, a deception. Consider how each of these reflects a false peace:

- A possession. Personal peace is a commodity defined and controlled by the possessor. Since peace is private and personal, it cannot be disputed or contested. Possessive peace is a one-way street with little or no concern for reconciliation with others. It is individualism and selfishness.

- An emotion. Emotional peace is a feeling, a state of mind, that may or may not have any relationship to truth and may change as quickly as it came.

- A deception. Deceptive peace ignores the deceitfulness of the human heart. It allows no room to test the peace against God's Word, His Spirit, and the affirmation of His people.

2. AGREEING TO DISAGREE

When Christians say, as they often do, "Let's agree to disagree," they reach for compromise instead of reconciliation, for independence instead of mutual submission. Agreeing to disagree can only lead to peace when the matters are not significant or essential. In this case, it is a matter of forbearance, not peace. Too often, Christians use "We're agreeing to disagree" as an excuse not to do the hard work of mutual submission and reconciliation.

Believers can no more agree to disagree about crucial matters in the church than players can agree to disagree about whether they are playing baseball or soccer on a field. To have any order or meaning, there must be agreement. Yet, in our work with conflicted churches, we frequently find believers opting to "agree to disagree" over fundamental values, goals, and mission. Some churches go so far as to promote their tolerance and celebrate their diversity as a virtue.

In Scripture, Christians are never called to agree to disagree. They are called to agree—in mutual submission under the lordship of Jesus Christ. Consider these two Scripture passages:

I appeal to you, brothers, in the name of our Lord Jesus Christ, that all of you agree with one another so that there may be no divisions among you and that you may be perfectly united in mind and thought. (1 Corinthians 1:10)

Therefore, my brothers, you whom I love and long for, my joy and crown, that is how you should stand firm in the Lord, dear friends! I plead with Euodia and I plead with Syntyche to agree with each other in the Lord. (Philippians 4:1–2)

Jesus links spiritual agreement on earth to heavenly fellowship, worship, and blessing. Jesus says, "Again, I tell you that if two of you on earth agree about anything you ask for, it will be done for you by my Father in heaven. For where two or three come together in my name, there am I with them" (Matthew 18:19). Note that these guidelines follow immediately after Jesus' instructions for confronting and reconciling sin.

Richard Baxter once said, "In necessary things, unity; in doubtful things, liberty; in all things, charity." We must agree on necessary things.

3. FORGIVING AND FORGETTING

Similarly, "forgive and forget" is a phrase used by believers who are impatient with God and with their fellow believers in the work of repentance, restitution, and restoration.

They say, "Let's get on with the business of the church," forgetting (ironically) that the work of the church is reconciliation; that is, transforming character. For many churches, however, reconciliation equals evasion—using "forgive and forget" to make the conflict go away. This undermines the cost and purpose of the Cross. God did not send His Son that we might forgive and forget. He sent His Son that we might be redeemed—changed.

The verse often quoted for "forgetting" is Paul's statement in Philippians, "But one thing I do: Forgetting what is behind and straining toward what is ahead, I press on toward the goal to win the prize for which God has called me heavenward in Christ Jesus" (Philippians 3:13–14). Christians use this as a proof text (and pretext) for ignoring past sins and moving into the future. The context of this passage, however, is not the apostle's desire to forget sin and move forward. Quite the opposite. Paul seeks to forget any "confidence in the flesh" that might lay claim to his redemption.

The apostle wants to "consider everything a loss compared to the surpassing greatness of knowing Christ Jesus my Lord." Further, it is his goal "to know Christ and the power of his resurrection and the fellowship of sharing in his sufferings, becoming like him in his death, and so, somehow, to attain to the resurrection from the dead" (vv. 8, 10). Paul is saying, "Remember the cross!" Jesus offers peace and reconciliation far greater than our ability to forget. Jesus offers an active, ongoing ability to "live at peace" with full restoration in Christ.

4. PEACEKEEPING

Many believers and churches confuse peacemaking with peace-keeping. Peacemaking is active and proactive. The peacemaker is committed to speaking the truth in love, to repenting, forgiving, and restoring. This is a biblical, redemptive response to conflict.

Peacekeeping is passive and reactive. In fact, as the title of chapter 5 implies, peacekeeping is the hallmark of passive responders (though aggressive and defensive responders also may practice this approach, as we will see). Peacekeepers often make the problem worse by enabling or ignoring sin in order to "make the problem go away."

Note peacekeepers can be both left- and right-handed. A peace-keeper can be passive, avoiding or evading conflict at every turn. Or a peacekeeper can force peace by attacking or defending.

Reconciling peace is made, not kept. Biblical peace is generative, life-giving. God calls the church into His redemptive process.

5. DÉTENTE

Détente is a relaxing of tension between rivals following a negotiation or agreement. However, détente is founded upon fundamental mistrust.

The word *détente* has been in use for nearly a century but came into common parlance in the Western world during the Cold War years between the former Soviet Union and the United States. Détente was a kind of reluctant coexistence—an uneasy peace founded upon treaties with one eye toward trade and one eye toward limiting the production and use of nuclear bombs. *Détente* meant sleeping with one nuclear eye open.

In the church, détente seeks to negotiate compromise without reconciling fundamental differences. We see this frequently in issues such as worship and the role of women. Churches practice détente when they become divided between traditional and contemporary forms of worship. Instead of coming together under God's Word and Spirit to discover what it means to worship in mutual submission, the church seeks appeasement by creating two services: a nine o'clock contemporary service and a traditional worship at eleven. Détente makes worship a matter of individual choice and personal preference.

One afternoon I received an E-mail from a member of a former church we had served. The church was rewriting its bylaws and had become mired in a disagreement over the role of women. Specifically, the church was debating whether a woman could serve as elder.

"What is your position on the role of women?" she asked me.

"I can think of few things that would be *less* helpful to you right now than your knowing my position on the role of women," I responded. "My opinion or your opinion means very little. It is the wrong question. Your question should be 'How has the church—the gathered community of faith down through the ages—interpreted God's Word and discerned God's Spirit on this issue?' Then, 'How do we understand God's voice today as we come in mutual submission under the lordship of Jesus Christ?'"

I went on to explain that orthodox faith communities have come to different biblical conclusions on the specific role of women—from a literal interpretation that forbids women any role in the church to a gift-based understanding that welcomes women serving in all positions. The specific conclusion a church comes to is less important than the church's faithfulness to God's Word and submission to His Spirit.

Here is where many churches today succumb to détente. The church holds to a high view of God's Word and decides that Scripture forbids women serving as elders. At the same time the church recognizes spiritual maturity and leadership gifts among several women in their congregation. To "reconcile" these two ideas, the church decides to form two boards: a board of elders comprised of men, and a governing board comprised of men and women (or, in some churches, a board of deaconesses to complement the board of deacons). Often, the two boards serve as coequals, or the governing board is above the elder board, thereby circumventing (and defeating) the church position on the role of women.

This is détente. Though sincere, it is neither reconciling nor honest. It is a false peace. Whenever a church comes to discern and affirm God's voice, it should be consistently obedient and faithful to follow His leading.

Détente in the church also occurs when leaders try to negotiate peace by sharing power. Here, churches construct boards and committees comprised of individuals who "represent" various sides of an issue in the same way democratic governments seek a balance of power. Each committee member serves like a congressman, representing a block of voters.

We served a church many years ago that decided to place people on the pastoral search committee who did not participate in or agree with the new church vision worked out over the previous eight months. When asked why they nominated people who were against the process, the leaders responded, "We wanted them to feel included . . . and to balance perspective."

As you might expect, the search team struggled to find a pastor they could agree upon. Eventually, the church called a pastor who promptly dismantled the church vision. In the first year, many key leaders went to talk with the pastor personally about the shared vision process and consensus reached in the church prior to his coming. Within two years, ten key leadership families had left the church in frustration.

Détente is an empty peace. In the church, peace comes by "re-presenting" Christ, not by representing opinions or points of view.

Churches practice détente when they refuse to confront a sin, or when they allow a sinner to resign or leave the church without confession or reconciliation. Reconciling peace requires confession.

Détente negotiates at the back door while Jesus stands at the front door knocking.

TRUE PEACE

In previous chapters, we have explored counterfeit ways we try to achieve peace. All come up empty because each is founded and guided by human emotion or control. To achieve true and lasting peace, we must turn to the One who is peace: Jesus Christ.

Peace is the fruit of living under the lordship of Jesus Christ. To be redemptive is, first and foremost, an act of obedience and submission.

ON BECOMING A REDEMPTIVE COMMUNITY

Why do we need a redemptive community—or even redemption? Because we all are sinners. In fact, the thrust of Scripture assumes two very important facts. First, all of us sin and fall short. All, including leaders, will fail—often miserably. You can take this fact to the bank. We are sinners. This is not surprising to God and should not surprise us. Second, and because of the first, God has provided a remedy for our sin in the life, death, and resurrection of Jesus Christ. Our cure is repentance.

Here, again, the Gospel turns conventional wisdom on its head. In Western, democratic culture, we are presumed innocent until proven guilty. All benefit of doubt is given to the sinner. The presumption of Scripture is the opposite. We—all of us—are guilty. What's more, the sinner is expected, even obligated, to turn himself in. In God's eyes, the sinner should be the first to expose his sin, even before it is commonly known. Consider these two commands:

Therefore, if you are offering your gift at the altar and there remember that your brother has something against you, leave your gift
there in front of the altar. First go and be reconciled to your brother;
then come and offer your gift. Settle matters quickly with your
adversary. (Matthew 5:23–25)

Therefore confess your sins to each other and pray for each other
so that you may be healed. The prayer of a righteous man is powerful and effective. (James 5:16)

What distinguishes the Christian story from others is that
God, in grace, provides the means for us to right our wrongs,
to take full responsibility for our sin and, in so doing, begin a
process of reconstituting our character, which led us to sin in
the first place. This means that the Gospel offers much more
than forgiveness. It promises transformation. Self-disclosure of
sin is the first step to transformation. The goal of reconciliation
is restoration and transformation. Making peace is the process
of bringing everything under the Light.

In part 3 we will see how the church comes alongside the
individual to assist in confession and restoration. From church
leaders, including the pastor, to the followers in the pews, we will
learn the mandate of submission and the spiritual blessings that
come when we submit (chapter 10). We learn how to confront
personal sin as well as sins of others in the local body and,
equally important, the proper responses to recognizing our sins:
confession and asking forgiveness (chapters 11–12). Finally, we
will consider how we reform the damaged community through
discipline and restitution (chapter 13).

Through it all, we are to be a redemptive community. Every
believer is called to be a peacemaker. Being redemptive is a way
of thinking; a way of life. Most believers do not think about

reconciliation until there is a conflict. Yet, reconciliation has been on God's heart and mind from the beginning of time. We are called into God's purpose, to be part of His redemptive will for the world.

Being redemptive, in contrast to being passive, evasive, defensive, or aggressive, requires a commitment to transformation under the lordship of Jesus Christ. It is a commitment to live and proclaim Truth—personally and corporately.

Being redemptive is a way of seeing. It is a set of habits and practices for living. That is, a peacemaker lives in such a way as to claim the lordship of Christ over all life, through the power of the Cross. Being redemptive proves grace.

I was leading a Bible study in a church that was suffering great pain because a former staff member was suing the church. We were discussing this when suddenly I heard myself saying, "This lawsuit is God's grace for you right now." Everyone grew silent. I continued to apply the lesson out loud. "God, in grace, has given you an opportunity to love a brother who is suing you while trusting God to vindicate truth and work out justice. Are you willing to live redemptively into that grace?"

We talked about this together. We reminded ourselves that being redemptive does not mean we negate or deny pain. Instead, being redemptive means asking questions such as, "What are we going to do with the pain?" "How can we learn and grow through the pain?" "What would it look like to respond redemptively?"

A redemptive perspective and posture changes our attitude toward conflict. When we declare the lordship of Christ and the power of the Cross over the conflicts, we still feel, but we need not fear, our pain or our failure. Being redemptive is not some form of positive thinking; it is not self-confidence or a "name it, claim it" approach to problem solving. Being redemptive is not a mind game where we become master of our circumstances.

Being redemptive changes nothing about the reality or threat of a conflict. In the church above, our conversation had no impact on the facts. The lawsuit stood. No one knew the outcome. It might destroy the church. The pain was real.

Being redemptive means saying, "It is what it is." Redemptive responders do not ignore or dwell on problems; they define current reality for what it is. Sin always stinks. God hates it. So should we. But He has given everything we need to be reconciled.

Being redemptive is living into and under the lordship of Jesus Christ. It is a way of placing our hardships (and our joys) under the Light so that we may see and respond to them redemptively. That is, reconciliation is not so much a collection of principles to be remembered or steps to be taken as it is an embodied way of life. (See 1 John 1:5; 2:9–10.) As the apostle John reminded us: "But if we walk in the light, as he is in the light, we have fellowship with one another, and the blood of Jesus, his Son, purifies us from all sin" (1 John 1:7).

In the next several chapters we will look at how God calls the church and all believers to a ministry of reconciliation under lordship and light. Before we examine these more closely, two principles bear mentioning briefly:

1. Everything you need to be reconciled has already been provided for you in God's Word, by His Spirit, and through His church.

2. Reconciliation must always involve all three: the Word, the Spirit, and the church.

First and foremost, God has given us His Word. The lordship of Christ is always connected to the Word of Christ. (For example, see Psalm 138:2.) Scripture is the authoritative, life-giving description of what it means to follow Christ truthfully. The writer to Hebrews declares God's Word to be "living and active. Sharper than any double-edged sword, it penetrates even to dividing soul and spirit, joints and marrow; it judges the thoughts and attitudes of the heart" (Hebrews 4:12).

To be redemptive requires submission to the authority of Scripture. It is the process of hearing and rightly interpreting God's truth (2 Timothy 2:15) in such a way that the church becomes a called-out people who are transformed by the power and wisdom of the resurrected Christ.

But how do we hear and interpret rightly? How do we avoid right-handed legalism or left-handed relativism? How do we distinguish God's will from human opinion?

Paul exhorted the Thessalonians to "test everything. Hold on to the good" (1 Thessalonians 5:21). Likewise, Paul admonished the Corinthians to "examine" and "test" themselves to see if Christ was in them (2 Corinthians 13:5). He commended the Berean believers for being of "noble character" because, in part, they "examined the Scripture to see if what Paul said was true" (Acts 17:11).

Like the Bereans, we are to test all teaching for consistency with all of God's Word. History is littered with the heresies of those who claimed Scripture as their authority. These heresies were exposed and corrected by the church interpreting Scripture by Scripture.

Yet, many church conflicts are about issues and ideas not specifically addressed in Scripture. How do we interpret Scripture and reconcile conflicts over differing philosophies or approaches to ministry, for example, or over issues such as style of worship, parenting, educating children, dating, or when to build a new facility?

How do we discern God's voice and follow His prompting in reconciliation? How do we know God's will when Scripture is silent or unclear?

Jesus gave the answer when He told His disciples, "I have much more to say to you, more than you can now bear. But when he, the Spirit of truth, comes, he will guide you into all truth" (John 16:12–13). (For more on the Spirit as revealer of truth, see also John 14:17, 26; 15:26; 1 Corinthians 2:10–13; 1 John 4:6.) The Holy Spirit's role is vital in resolving conflict and reaching reconciliation. The Bible can only be understood as it is heard, discerned, and lived in a disciplined community, under the guidance of the Holy Spirit.

With His Word and Spirit, God gives us the church. From the first church in Acts throughout the New Testament witness, the church is described as a community of faith. We are a people who are called to mutual love, to live and learn with one another, and to lift the name of Christ together. We are a body, a people of the Way.

Further, the community of faith is the place God has designated to "preach the Word . . . correct, rebuke and encourage" (2 Timothy 4:2). Discipline and discernment are given to the church to discern God's will and to work out reconciliation. Reconciliation is always about submission—to God's Word, His Spirit, and to one another—involving spiritual discernment that guards against objective legalism or subjective relativism.

The Word, the Spirit, and the church partner to bring about reconciliation within the fellowship of believers. Of these three, we can make several concluding observations:

~ Reconciliation is the work of God in Christ through submission to God's Word, the guidance of the Holy Spirit, and the discernment of the church.

- ∽ Efforts to reconcile church conflict based upon God's Word alone will inevitably become pharisaic or legalistic.
- ∽ Efforts to reconcile church conflict by experiencing God's Spirit alone will inevitably become subjective.
- ∽ Efforts to reconcile church conflict by the church consensus alone will inevitably become democratic.

To be redemptive, we must submit ourselves to the lordship of Jesus Christ under His Word, through His Spirit, and in His church.

Ten

LIVING UNDER LORDSHIP:
A CALL TO SUBMISSION

If we live, we live to the Lord; and if we die, we die to the
Lord. So, whether we live or die, we belong to the Lord.
For this very reason, Christ died and returned to life so
that he might be the Lord of both the dead and the living.

      ∾ ROMANS 14:8–9

In simplest terms, living under lordship means giving up control. The word *lord* is taken from a root word meaning "to sell" or "to be strong." Lordship refers to dominion; power; and authority, literally "having a power or authority," or "the power to control." Lordship recognizes absolute authority, absolute power. To call someone "lord" is to recognize jurisdiction over a territory; we yield control to the one in charge.

In the Greek Old Testament, the word *Lord* appears more than 6,000 times in reference to the Hebrew name for God. Lordship in Old Testament times meant absolute trust and dependence upon Yahweh. Scripture narrates the story of God creating and invading our life and history. Knowing God means having an encounter with and surrendering to His lordship.

The New Testament names Jesus Christ as the fulfillment of Old Testament prophecy. Jesus is King of Kings and Lord of Lords; He fulfills Yahweh's plan. At His name, every knee will bow, "in heaven and on earth and under the earth" (Philippians 2:10). Believers are followers of Jesus, who can do nothing apart from Him, but who can do all things in His Name. (See John 15:5 and Philippians 4:13.)

LORDSHIP AND SUBMISSION

Reconciliation is the process of bringing our lives—our differences, failures, sins, and fears—under the lordship of Jesus Christ. This is, first and foremost, an act of submission. The focus of our church leaders, therefore, should be submission to Christ and to one another.

The Greek word for *submit* literally means "to subject oneself to." It is a military term meaning "to arrange a troop or division in a military fashion under the command of a leader." In nonmilitary use, submission is "a voluntary attitude of giving in, cooperating, assuming responsibility, and carrying a burden."[1]

Biblical submission is related to our heart; it is unconditional. Submission is inward surrender governing outward action. In the church, submission begins with surrendering oneself to Christ and, in reverence for Him, to others. Without submission, there is no church. Specifically, reconciliation assumes and requires submission in three ways: to God, to one another, and to authority.

1. Submission to God. Submission is described as the obedient contrast to willful rebellion. Those who refuse to follow God's authority are called "stiff-necked" and "hostile." Submission to God is a sign of faith and requisite for forgiveness and life.[2] As the apostle James wrote, "Submit yourselves, then, to God. Resist the devil, and he will flee from you" (James 4:7).

2. Submission to one another. Submission is the mutuality command that, along with love, provides the foundation for all relationships in the church.[3] We looked at these "one another" commands in chapter 3. Forbearing, forgiving, serving, and all

other one-another commands assume a foundation of submission. Submitting to one another is an act of worship, because submission to others shows reverence for Christ (Ephesians 5:21). Submission is more than our duty to God; it is an act of worship guided by a heart for the Lord.[4]

3. Submission to authority. In Scripture, authority is a gift. Authority always resides in God, not man; it is never in man's power, position, or possession. Spiritual authority comes from, and points to, God. Authority demands humility and responsibility: humility, because both leader and follower are under God; responsibility, because God requires authority to be exercised and respected for the Lord's sake. "Everyone must submit himself to the governing authorities, for there is no authority except that which God has established. The authorities that exist have been established by God" (Romans 13:1).

THE EXAMPLE OF JESUS

While we expect God to require submission of His creation, we are amazed to find that He does so by example. The stunning image of the Gospel is the author of life submitting Himself to death and shame.[5] As the apostle Peter told onlookers near the temple: "You killed the author of life, but God raised him from the dead" (Acts 3:15)

In the life, death, and resurrection of Jesus we find the model of submission.

First, Jesus submitted to His Father's will. He told a crowd by the Sea of Galilee, "For I have come down from heaven not to do my will but to do the will of him who sent me (John 6:38). Much later, in the Garden of Gethsemane, Jesus prayed, "Father, if you are willing, take this cup from me; yet not my will, but yours be done" (Luke 22:42).

Second, Jesus modeled submission to His disciples. "Now that I, your Lord and Teacher, have washed your feet, you also should wash one another's feet" (John 13:14). Recall the scene in that upper room the night Jesus was betrayed. Jesus had gathered with those whose earthly lives meant the most to Him, and upon whose shoulders the Gospel would rest. Knowing the events about to unfold, Jesus humbled Himself and washed His disciples' feet, including the feet of the betrayer who sat with Him.

> When he had finished washing their feet, he put on his clothes and returned to his place. "Do you understand what I have done for you?" he asked them. "You call me 'Teacher' and 'Lord,' and rightly so, for that is what I am. Now that I, your Lord and Teacher, have washed your feet, you also should wash one another's feet. I have set you an example that you should do as I have done for you. I tell you the truth, no servant is greater than his master, nor is a messenger greater than the one who sent him. Now that you know these things, you will be blessed if you do them. (John 13:12–17)

Submission is requisite for spiritual blessing.

Third, Jesus laid down any claim to Sonship by submitting to Pilate's authority. "No one takes it from me, but I lay it down of my own accord," Jesus declared. "I have authority to lay it down and authority to take it up again. This command I received from my Father" (John 10:18). When Pilate urged Jesus to answer his questions, citing his power as Roman governor to free Him, Jesus answered, "You would have no power over me if it were not given to you from above" (John 19:11).

THE SUBMISSIVE LEADER: HUMBLE, LEADABLE, TEACHABLE

While submission will reveal itself in many ways, three specific traits mark the submissive leader. A leader who is submissive to Christ, to others, and to the church will be humble, leadable, and teachable.

We are often asked for advice by pastoral search committees in how to find and select the "right" pastor. We always recommend that a church hire on the basis of character first and skills second. Spiritual brokenness is always the first attribute to look for. If a candidate for pastor cannot demonstrate spiritual brokenness, he should not be invited to be the senior position. Never call a leader who is not humble, leadable, and teachable.

As I write these words, the images of three pastors come to mind, each of whom we interviewed in the past year. All had been fired from their churches, or left their churches unreconciled.

When we asked each pastor, "What have you learned from this experience?" or, "What would you do differently next time?" each gave responses that revealed his character. All of the "lessons" mentioned were self-absorbed and defensive; each blamed or accused others for the problems in the church. Not one of these leaders could think of something he would do differently. Each refused reconciliation.

These negative attributes are easy to see in others, but how do you measure up? Are you humble, leadable, and teachable? Perhaps you have come to view such traits as a barrier to success. *After all, who wants to follow someone weak?* you may think.

Here, again, we are surprised that God Himself is first to model these traits in His Son. What's more, He calls us to follow likewise.

THE SUBMISSION OF JESUS

JESUS WAS HUMBLE.

It is hard to imagine a more humble entry and exit of a messiah. Consider how the prophet Isaiah described the Messiah. He was "despised and rejected by men, a man of sorrows, and familiar with suffering. Like one from whom men hide their faces he was despised, and we esteemed him not. . . . He was oppressed and afflicted, yet he did not open his mouth. . . . He was assigned a grave with the wicked" (Isaiah 53:3, 7, 9). These are hardly words one would expect to describe the Messiah, sent from God.

From the Incarnation to the Crucifixion, the story of Jesus is nothing short of scandalous to human ears and modern notions of leadership. The Son of God was born in a feed trough and lived a life of obscurity followed by betrayal, public ridicule, and finally death on a cursed cross. "They spit in his face and struck him with their fists. Others slapped him. . . . Those who passed by hurled insults at him, shaking their heads (Matthew 26:67; 27:39). Christ's response? According to the Scriptures, "when they hurled their insults at him, he did not retaliate; when he suffered, he made no threats. Instead, he entrusted himself to him who judges justly" (1 Peter 2:23).

This is not the biography of a hero. This is not what leadership manuals promote. To the one who would lead, Jesus would say, "No servant is greater than his master, nor is a messenger greater than the one who sent him. Now that you know these things, you will be blessed if you do them" (John 13:16–17). Indeed, any who would follow after Christ should expect to suffer. "To this you were called, because Christ suffered for you, leaving you an example, that you should follow in his steps" (1 Peter 2:21).

JESUS WAS LEADABLE.

Prior to His public ministry and following His baptism, Jesus, full of the Holy Spirit, "was led by the Spirit into the desert to be tempted by the devil" (Matthew 4:1). This passage is remarkable in many ways, not least of which is Jesus' submission to the leading of the Spirit. To be full of the Spirit is to be in full submission to God, under God's control. Jesus was led into the desert to be tempted.

Later, Jesus would teach His disciples to pray, "Lead us not into temptation, but deliver us from evil." Jesus knew what it meant to be led. He knew what it meant to be tempted, particularly the temptation to claim for personal benefit the power granted by the Father.

He ate nothing during those [forty] days, and at the end of them he was hungry. The devil said to him, "If you are the Son of God, tell this stone to become bread." Jesus answered, "It is written: 'Man does not live on bread alone.'" The devil led him up to a high place and showed him in an instant all the kingdoms of the world. And he said to him, "I will give you all their authority and splendor, for it has been given to me, and I can give it to anyone I want to. So if you worship me, it will all be yours." Jesus answered, "It is written: 'Worship the Lord your God and serve him only.'" The devil led him to Jerusalem and had him stand on the highest point of the temple. "If you are the Son of God," he said, "throw yourself down from here. For it is written: 'He will command his angels concerning you to guard you carefully; they will lift you up in their hands, so that you will not strike your foot against a stone.'" Jesus answered, "It says: 'Do not put the Lord your God to the test.'" (Luke 4:2–12)

This stands in stark contrast to many who would claim knowledge, position, or spiritual status as their justification to lead others. George Shultz, former Secretary of State in the Reagan administration, once said about leadership, "Never give great responsibility to someone who cannot live without it." A man must be leadable before he is fit to lead.

Can you live without responsibility, position, or control? Can you lead without coercion? (Influence by force is coercion, not leadership.)

JESUS WAS TEACHABLE.

Perhaps most remarkable or surprising is that Jesus was teachable. Scripture affirms that Jesus Christ was fully God and fully man. Jesus lacked nothing in knowledge or wisdom. Yet, Jesus learned. He experienced all the ambiguity and pain of humanity, yet without sin.

Specifically, Hebrews explains, "During the days of Jesus' life on earth, he offered up prayers and petitions with loud cries and tears to the one who could save him from death, and he was heard because of his reverent submission. Although he was a son, he learned obedience from what he suffered" (5:7–8).

"In bringing many sons to glory," the writer to the Hebrews said, "it was fitting that God, for whom and through whom everything exists, should make the author of their salvation perfect through suffering" (2:10). This means Jesus is able to sympathize with our weaknesses. "We have one who has been tempted in every way, just as we are—yet was without sin. Let us then approach the throne of grace with confidence, so that we may receive mercy and find grace to help us in our time of need" (4:15–16).

SUBMISSION AND OBEDIENCE

The relationship of submission to obedience is a common point of contention and misunderstanding in the church. In some churches, these terms have become equivalent to malevolent and abusive leadership. Legalistic requirements for obedience or submission amount to spiritual manipulation or coercion. Yet, Scripture calls the church and all believers to submit and to obey. This prompts several questions:

- How do submission and obedience relate to lordship and leadership?
- How and when are we to obey?
- Is there biblical cause to disobey a leader; is there ever cause to rebel?
- Should we submit to leaders who are clearly sinning or hurting the congregation?

OBEDIENCE MEANS ACTION

Earlier in this chapter we discovered that submission is about our attitude, a matter of the heart. We will soon see that obedience is about action, a matter of faith. In fact, the Hebrew and Greek words translated "obey" in Scripture carry a sense of response. The hearer hears, understands, and obeys. Hearing implies doing. Obedience is the response of the believer to truth.

In the New Testament, the apostle Paul and the writer to the Hebrews exhort readers to obey and submit to leaders:

> Remind the people to be subject to rulers and authorities, to be obedient, to be ready to do whatever is good. (Titus 3:1)

> Obey your leaders and submit to their authority. They keep watch over you as men who must give an account. Obey them so that their work will be a joy, not a burden, for that would be of no advantage to you. (Hebrews 13:17)

The clear teaching of Scripture is that leaders are to be honored and obeyed. Yet, both the Old and New Testaments give stories of faithful men and women who deliberately disobeyed authority in order to obey God.

For example, in the first chapter of Exodus, Hebrew midwives disobeyed Pharaoh's order to kill all newborn boys (Exodus 1:15–19). The midwives were honored for "fearing God" when they protected the newborns' lives (vv. 20–21). In the Book of Daniel, Shadrach, Meshach, and Abednego disobeyed Nebuchadnezzar's order to bow down and worship the image of gold. Later in the same book, Daniel disobeyed the king's decree by praying (3:4–18; 6:6–16). In the New Testament, Peter and the other apostles twice defied the orders of the Sanhedrin to stop preaching the Gospel, saying, "Judge for yourselves whether it is right in God's sight to obey you rather than God," and, "We must obey God rather than men!" (Acts 4:19; 5:29).

In each of the stories above, believers disobeyed, yet they submitted to the proper authority. When Shadrach, Meshach, and Abednego were brought before King Nebuchadnezzar and given another chance to bow down, they replied, in effect, "We submit to your authority to burn us alive, but we will not bow down," ending their statement with "If we are thrown into the blazing furnace, the God we serve is able to save us from it, and he will rescue us from your hand, O king. But even if he does not, we want you to know, O king, that we will not serve your gods or worship the image of gold you have set up" (Daniel 3:17–18).

SUBMISSION IS UNCONDITIONAL

Scripture teaches that obedience to man is required unless it violates God's commands. Having learned this, we would expect a similar conditional rule for submission. But when we look for exceptions, we find none. In fact, we may be somewhat surprised to find that submission is required even in the face of obvious failure or sin.

For example, in the Book of Genesis we read how Noah became drunk and fell asleep naked on the floor. Noah's son, Ham, discovered his father uncovered and told his brothers. Shem and Japheth entered the room respectfully to cover Noah's shame. Ham was cursed for his rebellion (Genesis 9:20–27). In the Book of Numbers, Moses clearly defied God's law by marrying a Cushite woman, yet when Aaron and Miriam spoke against him, claiming God spoke to them as well, God struck Miriam with leprosy (12:1–10). Later, when Korah, Dathan, and Abiram rebelled against Moses and Aaron, criticizing them for taking too much upon their shoulders, the earth opened up and swallowed the three men. When the people grumbled against Moses, God struck them with a plague (16:1–35; 41–50). In the New Testament, Jesus and the disciples repeatedly recognized and submitted to the secular and religious authorities.

The witness of Scripture is that submission is unconditional. Noah and Moses had clearly sinned against God. Yet, God requires believers to submit independent of the sin or failure of the authority. In fact, leadership failure is the true test of submission. Why? Because submission reveals lordship; submission reveals the heart.

It is easy to submit to people we like or believe in. Our heart is revealed by how we submit when a leader is wrong, or injustice is being done. This is a hard teaching because it strikes at the heart of our independence and autonomy.

Once, we received a call from a man in a church where the senior pastor had brought great harm to his congregation through spiritual abuse and intimidation. He was clearly in the wrong. "What should I do?" the man asked me. "Go and confront the pastor," I replied. "I did that, and now he is attacking me," he explained. "Go back with a witness," I counseled. He did this, but to no avail. "Ask the elders to help you be reconciled," I recommended.

Weeks later, the man called back, explaining that the elders and the pastor had refused to meet with him. Instead, the pastor had removed him from ministry and accused him of being divisive. When he asked for a meeting to hear what he had done wrong and to reconcile how he had sinned, the pastor refused to meet with him. The pastor demanded that the man submit to his authority. "What should I do now?" he asked. "You have two options," I replied. "You can stay in the church and be quiet, asking God to work vindication, or you can leave the church quietly. In either case, you must submit."

"But it isn't right," the man exclaimed. I agreed. He went on to explain his concern about other people being hurt. I shared his concern.

We talked about the issues involved. The leader was sinning and hurting people. The man was not responsible for the leader's sin. In fact, the leader had a bigger problem; the pastor was accountable to God.

The man's responsibility was to honor and submit to the leader out of reverence for Christ. He was responsible for confronting the pastor in love, following the steps of Matthew 18. He was not responsible for the pastor's reaction or response, or for his refusing reconciliation. He was responsible to do all he could to be at peace. He was accountable for his own heart and actions. This meant he must not talk to others. He must not take authority that was not his. He must submit.

Scripture teaches that submission is related to the heart; it is unconditional. We submit to authority in reverence to Christ. Rebellion is never God's will or way. Obedience is related to our conduct; it is conditional upon God's command. God's authority is sovereign and must receive unqualified obedience. Man's authority is delegated and must receive qualified obedience. Obedience is outward action guided by inner faith. Submission is inner heart governing outward action.

Most church conflict is about submission, not obedience. Without submission there is no church.

Notes

1. Geoffrey Bromiley, ed., *Theological Dictionary of the New Testament* (Grand Rapids: Eerdmans, 1985), 1156.
2. 2 Chronicles 30:8; Romans 8:7; 10:3; Hebrews 12:9.
3. Philippians 2:3; 1Peter 2:17; 5:5.
4. Romans 13:1–5; Hebrews 12:9; James 4:7;1 Peter 2:13–18.
5. Hebrews 2:10; 12:2.

Eleven

LIVING INTO THE LIGHT:
WHY WE MUST EXAMINE AND CONFRONT

*For you were once darkness, but now you are light in the
Lord. Live as children of light (for the fruit of the light
consists in all goodness, righteousness and truth) and find
out what pleases the Lord. Have nothing to do with the
fruitless deeds of darkness, but rather expose them.*

~ EPHESIANS 5: 8–11

Throughout the Gospels, Jesus contrasts light and darkness.
Light is Christ Himself (John 8:12; 12:46). Light is the symbol of
obedience and faith (John 3:19–21) and spiritual purity (1 John
1:5). Darkness represents spiritual separation, depravity, and cor-
ruption. Light and darkness are not passive states but active agents,
leading in opposite directions.

The apostle Paul reminds us that we are saved out of darkness
and are to "live as children of light" (Ephesians 5:8–9), echoing the
words of Jesus, "You are the light of the world. A city on a hill cannot be hidden" (Matthew 5:14).

Therefore, we ought to live as children of light. The temptation
is to hear Paul's words about light as some kind of spiritual status
that, once attained, remains. Instead, Paul describes an active, ongoing process of living into the light. We must be ever and always

bringing our personal and collective lives under the lordship and into the light of Jesus Christ.

This calling runs smack against our cultural ideals.

IS SIN A PRIVATE ISSUE?

Paul suggests that the church is a place where believers are called to continually expose sin in themselves and in one another. This offends our notion of democracy and privacy. We have come to believe, even celebrate, that we own our lives. If we have secret sins or dark parts of our lives, these are personal and private.

This idea of rights and ownership is destructive because it fosters the prevalent assumption that sin is our possession, something we can choose to keep to ourselves. For some, the sin even becomes part of their identity or self-understanding. We have seen this repeatedly in the church's avoidance and treatment of addictive behaviors, particularly sexual sin.

In most of the churches we have served, pornography has been revealed as a secret sin of a leader or member. In nearly all cases, the sinner minimizes the sin by claiming it is "private" and "does not hurt anyone." This is the lie of darkness. Pornography has a devastating impact on the sinner and those around him, who are degraded as objects, rather than treated as children of God. No sin is innocent or harmless, least of all sexual sin.

We find the same twisted reasoning from men and women practicing homosexual or heterosexual sin. When confronted, the sinner claims, "My private life is none of your business," or that others "have no right to judge." One man with a sexual addiction told us that we had no right to say anything to him until we had "walked in his shoes." This line of reasoning increases darkness, even invites others to join in. The sinner becomes increasingly blinded by, and in bondage to, his own perversity.

Darkness increases blindness. This is why Paul insists that all sin must be made visible. The church is called to expose darkness, to bring all secret sin into, and under, the light. In Scripture, sin is never private. Further, we do not possess sin; sin possesses us.

Living into the light is a personal and corporate command: "Live as children of light" (Ephesians 5:8). All sin, especially secret sin, always impacts the whole body because it breaks oneness in the same way adultery breaks oneness and sabotages a marriage long before the sin is known. The church, like marriage, is called to a fruitful life. Living into light produces a people who have hearts that are upright and lives that have integrity and purity. Living into light both produces and reveals truth, things as they really are. Only in the light can we live and communicate with authenticity.

Concealing sin is destructive and deceitful. Paul admonished the Ephesian church to "have nothing to do with the fruitless deeds of darkness." That is, believers are to have no fellowship, no partnership with the barren and unproductive deeds of darkness.

EXPOSING SIN

In effect, Paul said, "Turn the light on your sin." Whenever the believer is confronted with sin or darkness, he or she is to expose it.

The Greek word translated "expose" in Ephesians 5:11 is the same word used in several other key texts concerning reconciliation. For instance, in Matthew 18:15, Jesus instructed the believer, "If your brother sins against you, go and show him his fault [literally, "expose his sin"] just between the two of you. If he listens to you, you have won your brother over." Similarly, Paul instructed Timothy that church leaders are to be "exposed," or rebuked publicly, when they sin. Jesus told His disciples that a primary work of the Holy Spirit will be to "expose," or convict, the world of sin (1 Timothy 5:20; John 16:8).

In the previous chapter we learned how living under lordship requires unconditional submission to God, to authority, and to others. Christian community is founded upon and requires mutual commitment to live as children of the light. This is a prerequisite for

biblical worship, fellowship, and discipleship. This is communion—
a people sharing common devotion for, and mutual submission to,
the light of Jesus Christ.

All redemptive responses must start here—with Christian community—because the very meaning of words such as *reconciliation,
redemption,* and *restoration* assume a prior fellowship.

WHAT RECONCILIATION AND RESTORATION MEAN

In Scripture, the Greek word for *reconciliation* is an economic
term meaning "to exchange." To reconcile means the adjustment of
a difference on a balance sheet. In the New Testament, reconciliation restores sinners who repent and place their trust in the saving
work of Christ.[1] Christ's death pays for the price of sin.

The English word *reconcile* comes from the Latin root *conciliare,*
meaning "to draw or bring together; to unite," according to *Webster's
Revised Unabridged Dictionary.* Thus *reconciliation* means joining
together previously separate parts, reestablishing close relationships.
To reconcile is to settle or resolve anything that separates.

Scripture tells us that the goal of reconciliation is always restoration. In Galatians 6:1, Paul exhorts the spiritually mature in a church
to restore gently. It is stated as a command. The Greek word Paul
chooses for *restore* is the same used for mending fishing nets in
Matthew 4:21, meaning "to perfect," "make fit," or "to equip thoroughly." To restore is to make like new.

RECOVERY AND COMMUNITY

As the definitions above demonstrate, the words *reconcile* and
restore both point to recovery of what has been lost. Each presumes
a former state of community fellowship now separated or threatened
by sin. Darkness has crept in, and the light must be restored.

Yet, this is where many church efforts to be redemptive fail before
even getting started. They fail because they seek to restore some-

thing that was never present. The fact is we cannot restore sinners to fellowship where there is no fellowship.

Understanding this truth begins to explain why so many churches are in conflict and why so few are able to achieve full, biblical reconciliation. Our churches neither nurture nor practice genuine biblical community—actively living into and intentionally being transformed by the light. We lack the vibrant life of a people joined, heart and mind, under the lordship of Christ. We have forgotten, or never experienced, the fruit of a normal, Spirit-filled church: reverent worship, deep learning, common confession, intercessory prayer, and caring fellowship. We have drifted so far that we are surprised that this ought to be "normal."

Darkness critically impairs our ability to be reconciled. When a church fails to live fully in the light, that church has neither the skill, understanding, nor argument to "restore" a sinner. What would we be restoring the sinner to? What does restoration offer if our community life is superficial, or if our light turns out to be shadows?

Many years ago I asked a man in a church to confess his sin so that he might be restored to the local body. "Why should I?" the man replied. "No one else is honest about their sin." We do not have to agree with his logic to see the point: Biblical reconciliation requires genuine community.

This is the failure continually made in the church: We claim to know but fail to embody who we are in Christ. This is why biblical peacemaking principles and curriculums lack the power to change us; they inform but ultimately fail because they address our intellect, not our character.

Being redemptive calls for more than knowing what God says about reconciliation or how to do it. Being redemptive necessitates a way of life. It is more than applying the biblical principles of confession, confrontation, and discipline whenever a conflict emerges. It is embodying these specific habits and practices in one-another community.

To test this in your church, think about when, in the past few years, a sinner was taken through the full process of discipline, confession, forgiveness, restitution, and restoration. How many times has this happened? If your church is typical, the full process of restoration has seldom, if ever, happened. Either the process was shortened, or the sinner left the church.

We need to ask ourselves several questions: Why don't we follow the clear principles of Scripture for exposing sin and restoring the sinner? What is it about our church that believers would rather leave us than be restored to us? What does this say about our fellowship?

For the apostle Paul, there were only two worlds: the kingdom of light, where Jesus is Lord and believers joyfully gather in His name; and the kingdom of darkness, where Satan enslaves and destroys. So, when Paul recommended, as he did to the Corinthians, that an unrepentant sinner be put "out of your fellowship," he did so with the assumption that handing "this man over to Satan" would so shock the sinner that he would come to his senses and rush back into the light of Christian fellowship and forgiveness. (See 1 Corinthians 5:1–5.)

Reconciliation is the process of exposing sin and restoring the sinner to the light. Here again, the church must avoid the extremes of legalism and relativism. We must never expose sin for the sake of punishment or shame, but neither should privacy or fear of hurt keep us from confrontation. All reconciliation must be restorative—always truthful and always loving.

RECOVERY AND COMMUNICATION

To expose sin in redemptive and restorative ways, the church must practice authentic community. Authentic community requires authentic communication.

Authentic communication is "speaking the truth in love." The apostle Paul says it this way:

Instead, speaking the truth in love, we will in all things grow up into him who is the Head, that is, Christ. From him the whole body, joined and held together by every supporting ligament, grows and builds itself up in love, as each part does its work. . . . Therefore each of you must put off falsehood and speak truthfully to his neighbor, for we are all members of one body. (Ephesians 4:15–16, 25)

Authentic communication is the process of speaking the truth in love to others while inviting others to speak truth into our lives.

"These are the things you are to do: Speak the truth to each other, and render true and sound judgment in your courts; do not plot evil against your neighbor, and do not love to swear falsely. I hate all this," declares the Lord. (Zechariah 8:16–17)

Rather, we have renounced secret and shameful ways; we do not use deception, nor do we distort the word of God. On the contrary, by setting forth the truth plainly we commend ourselves to every man's conscience in the sight of God. (2 Corinthians 4:2)

AUTHENTIC COMMUNICATION: TRUTH AND LOVE

The words *community, communion,* and *communicate* all come from the same Greek root word, *koinonia,* meaning to "hold things in common," or "joint participation," most commonly translated as "fellowship." Community and communication are inseparable. You cannot have one without the other.

Christian communication stands in contrast to the world by its content (truth) and character (love). Our words ought always and only to build up wisdom and foster fellowship. This is not to say that hard things cannot or should not be spoken. In fact, speaking the truth in love requires saying hard words in loving ways. Leaders are admonished to correct, rebuke, and encourage. Speaking the truth often requires confrontation, yet always toward gentle restoration.

TRUTH AND LOVE DEFINED

In Scripture, the Greek word for *truth* is *aletheia,* which literally means "nonconcealment." Etymologically, the word denotes what is seen, indicated, expressed, or disclosed. Truth is things as they really are, not as concealed or falsified.

Scripture speaks of truth as the incarnation of Jesus Christ. We know God through the person of Jesus Christ. Faith comes by hearing. In fact, truth is an indwelling: Truth so inhabits us through the power of the Holy Spirit that we are guided "into" both speaking and living out truth. Truth is an encounter with Jesus Christ. Jesus told Pilate, "For this I came into the world, to testify to the truth. Everyone on the side of truth listens to me" (John 18:37).

Truth in the New Testament has to do with *being* as much as *knowing.* Scripture links truth with righteousness, uprightness, trustworthiness, and honesty. We might define truth as the attributes of mind and character that are free from affection, pretense, simulation, falsehood, or deceit. Being true is being genuine, being authentic. Truth is more than making right statements. It is "living out" a new reality only possible through the empowering presence of the Holy Spirit.

The Greek word for *love* is *agape,* meaning "total commitment and total trust."[2] Love is the sum of all commands and the true sign of believing faith. Love is our connection to the Father and an expression of our relationship with His Son. Jesus told His disciples, "As the Father has loved me, so have I loved you. Now remain in my love. If you obey my commands, you will remain in my love, just as I have obeyed my Father's commands and remain in his love" (John 15:9–10).

Then Jesus described the greatest example of love. "Greater love has no one than this, that he lay down his life for his friends" (John 15:13).

Truth and love are incarnational. When the "word became flesh," Jesus lived into perfect truth and perfect love. Jesus said, "I am the

Way, the Truth, and the Life. No one comes to the Father but by me" (John 1:14; 14:6). The apostle John wrote, "This is how we know what love is: Jesus Christ laid down his life for us. And we ought to lay down our lives for our brothers" (1 John 3:16).

WHAT TRUTH AND LOVE DO

Truth and love work together: Truth sanctifies; love sacrifices.

Jesus prayed for His disciples (and all disciples who would follow) "Sanctify them by the truth; your word is truth" (John 17:17). The Greek word for *sanctify* means "to make pure." Literally, Jesus is asking the Father to clean us up, make us pure by His Word. Truth has a purifying effect on our lives.

Love sacrifices. John writes, "This is love: not that we loved God, but that he loved us and sent his Son as an atoning sacrifice for our sins. Dear friends, since God so loved us, we also ought to love one another" (1 John 4:10–11). God's love is a sacrificial love. It is unselfish and unconditional.

Paul says that living in the light means a commitment to speak sanctifying truth with sacrificial love. The literal translation of Ephesians 4:15 would be "truthing in love." That is, Paul is referring to more than our words. To be "truthing" means our very lives together ought to be characterized by truth and love. Truth without love is not truth. Love without truth is not love. This is vital to understand. Remember, right-handed leaders tend to emphasize truth; left-handed, love. To be redemptive, we must have both.

Paul helps us see how being redemptive is indelibly linked to a peculiar kind of community practicing a specific kind of communication. It is a unified community, sharing "one hope . . . one Lord, one faith, one baptism; one God and Father of all, who is over all and through all and in all" (4:5–6). This was why grace was apportioned in gifts to the church, so that leaders could "prepare God's people for works of service" that will further unity and fullness in Christ (Ephesians 4:12).

We are called to live and grow into our faith. Standing still, then, is actually losing ground—drifting out from under lordship or sinking back into darkness. In Ephesians 4:14, Paul pictured an infant in a boat. We are as helpless to discern or reason spiritually as an infant would be helpless to captain the vessel. In contrast to this, the church is to grow up into Christ by "speaking the truth in love."

Note how the apostle has linked authentic spiritual growth to authentic communication. Our capacity to grow, Paul wrote, is directly related to our ability to see and to accept the truth about ourselves.

The Role of Community in Knowing Truth

This raises two immediate principles about the relationship of truth to individual believers and the need for the body of Christ. *First,* Paul assumed that *truth cannot be known completely by oneself.* We do not possess truth. We hear, learn, and respond to truth as it is revealed through God's Word, His Spirit, and the church. Not one of us knows the truth completely. Rather, we are invited into relationship with the One who is Truth. Truth is proved by the light.

This is a very important distinction. When a brother or sister claims that "God told me" something, we must treat the statement with the utmost respect and caution. Respect, because God can and does speak through His people. Caution, because our hearts are so self-deceiving[3] that we often cannot distinguish what is of God and what is of ourselves. Truth must always be tested, always brought into the light.

This is the work of faith, interpreting and proving God's Word in community. It protects us from spiritual arrogance on the one hand and spiritual charlatans on the other.

Second, if truth cannot be known completely by oneself, then *we cannot know the truth about ourselves by ourselves.* To see the truth about ourselves we need others to speak into our life. All of us have blind spots and weaknesses that keep us from seeing ourselves truthfully. Therefore, we need others who are committed to speak the truth in love.

Being authentic requires that we recognize the truth, accept the truth, and are able to change as a result of the truth. Authentic communication is transforming.

TRUTHFUL EXAMINATION

Being redemptive starts with examining self; bringing the truth about ourselves into the light.

To examine means answering pointed questions about your thoughts, feelings, motivations, and actions in a given conflict. Examination means testing your judgment and fruit.

> Do not judge, and you will not be judged. Do not condemn, and you will not be condemned. Forgive, and you will be forgiven. Give, and it will be given to you. A good measure, pressed down, shaken together and running over, will be poured into your lap. For with the measure you use, it will be measured to you. . . . Why do you look at the speck of sawdust in your brother's eye and pay no attention to the plank in your own eye? How can you say to your brother, "Brother, let me take the speck out of your eye," when you yourself fail to see the plank in your own eye? You hypocrite, first take the plank out of your eye, and then you will see clearly to remove the speck from your brother's eye. No good tree bears bad fruit, nor does a bad tree bear good fruit. Each tree is recognized by its own fruit. (Luke 6:37–38, 41–43)

Jesus' point was not, as some argue, a spiritual way of saying, "Mind your own business." He was not using threats or guilt to quiet criticism. Rather, Jesus was teaching about the reciprocal nature of reconciliation. A commitment to speak into the lives of others assumes a prior humility and vulnerability—a commitment to examine yourself. Paul wrote about this same mutuality in his instructions to the Galatians: "If someone is caught in a sin, you who are spiritual should restore him gently. But watch yourself, or you also may be tempted. Carry each other's burdens, and in this way you will fulfill the law of Christ. If anyone thinks he is something when he is nothing, he deceives himself" (6:1–3).

Earlier we learned that sin is never private. Here, we understand how all sin in the church is our sin. If there is a conflict or problem in the body of Christ, it is *our* problem. Indeed, we may be contributing to the very problem we seek to correct, perhaps more than we know. In fact, Jesus says, the fruit of our culpability is obvious to others, like a wooden plank that knocks people over each time we turn.

So Jesus says, "Do not judge." There is no contradiction in Jesus' teaching that it is never right for an individual believer to judge another, while Paul teaches that judgment is the corporate discernment and work of the church.[4] Judging sin is for the church, not the individual.

To be redemptive, Jesus says, you must start with spiritual examination.

We assume by Jesus' words that we are to conduct this examination by ourselves. Jesus is helping us become better at confrontation by making sure we look in our own spiritual mirror first. In this way we can avoid the charge of hypocrisy. But this is not Jesus' point. Instead, Jesus is reminding us how connected we are to others and how our sin is separating us from others. We are blinded by our own darkness. "The eye is the lamp of the body," Jesus says earlier in this Sermon on the Mount. Each of us must watch out, because "if your eyes are bad, your whole body will be full of darkness. If then the light within you is darkness, how great is that darkness!" (Matthew 6:23). To see our brother clearly we must move ourselves into the light.

WHERE TO START? WHAT TO ASK?

Examination precedes confrontation. When an issue of conflict arises, it is best to start by making three assertions. *First, admit, "I don't know what the problem is."* Even if you are sure what the problem is, start with the assumption that you may be wrong. Assuming that you know the problem may keep you from the fundamental issue God wants to heal. Assuming you do not know is the first step in finding and reconciling the real issue.

This concept, we have found, is very difficult for pastors. Like doctors, pastors are trained to know all the answers. One pastor in a conference told me, "I would never admit that I did not know something. They are paying me to know."

The most powerful call a leader can ever give to the church is a call to faith in the absence of certainty. "I don't know. Will you walk with me in faith?" Address a conflict or issue by reminding yourself you do not know the truth completely.

Second, the leader should say, "I must be contributing to the conflict somehow." This is what it means to live in community. "If there is an issue, I am part of it and likely contributing to the problem somehow."

Third, every leader faced with a conflict or issue should assert, "The problem that has surfaced is likely not the fundamental problem." Other factors likely exist that we do not know and have not surfaced yet that will help us understand.

Making these assertions is a way of examining self and putting perspective on the problem so that the real, fundamental issue can be exposed.

The leader must ask, "What is the real problem?" or, "What is it about me, my behavior, my relationships, my position, my beliefs, that this event is happening?" and, "How am I contributing to this problem?"

Examination starts with the assumption that there is a plank in your eye.

WHAT YOU CAN DO ABOUT PERSONAL SIN

There are two practical ways to examine your life and move into light. First, submit to God's Spirit; then, submit to His people.

SUBMIT TO GOD'S SPIRIT

Ask God, by His Holy Spirit, to reveal truth in your life. Read and meditate on Psalms 32 and 51. Then ask yourself the following question: "Is there anything in my life right now that, if it were to be exposed today, would bring dishonor to Jesus Christ, my marriage, or my ministry?"[5]

If you can answer yes to the question, let me suggest several truths for you to consider. First, sin is already separating you from God, others, and your ministry. Your sin is impacting your worship and fellowship. As Paul warned the Corinthians, a person "ought to examine himself before he eats of the bread and drinks of the cup" (1 Corinthians 11:28). Second, it is very likely that discerning people in the body already know or will know something is amiss. You can't hide. It is not a question of *if* you will be found out, but *when*. Your sin will find you out (Numbers 32:23). Third, God wants you to be freed, forgiven, and restored.

As God reveals darkness, step into the light by going immediately to two or three people to whom you can confess your sin and discern God's direction for you to repent, make restitution, and work out reconciliation.

SUBMIT TO GOD'S PEOPLE

Sometimes we are so blinded to our own darkness that we need others to examine us. Submission to God's people can help move us to the light. This may be done with a small group Bible study or in an accountability group. The people you ask should be those you worship and fellowship with—people with whom you already share community.

What You Can Do About Others' Sin: Loving Confrontation

The first step into light is truthfully examining and exposing your personal sin. The second step is lovingly confronting others who are in darkness. The greater the practice of biblical community, the more effective confrontation will be. Confrontation without community is not loving.

The Progression

The gospel of Matthew gives specific instructions about what a believer should do when made aware of sin. Whether we are the sinner or the one sinned against, Jesus says we must "go" (Matthew 5:23–24; 18:15). We are to go to the brother quickly, personally, and privately. The initiative is first with the singular personal, "I," then with the plural corporate, "you." The first step is always to go directly to resolve a sin one on one.

If the sin cannot be reconciled personally, bring witnesses. If that fails, exposing darkness becomes a matter for the church (18:15–17).

Note that the key word determining reconciliation is *listen*. Jesus said, "If he listens to you, you have won your brother over" (v. 15). Matthew 18 allows for just two possible reactions to a confrontation of sin by the sinner. The first is listening, with sincere action taken by the sinner to repent and/or to right the offense. This is living in the light. The second response is not listening: denying or taking defensive action to protect self. This is a decision to stay in darkness. Scripture calls an unwillingness to listen and live into the light as "stiff-necked" rebellion. Indeed, God said of Israel and Judah, "They would not listen and were as stiff-necked as their fathers, who did not trust in the LORD their God" (2 Kings 17:14).[6]

THREE PRINCIPLES FOR CONFRONTING

These instructions for the church living into the light offer three principles for loving confrontation.

First, the initiative for confronting sin is both personal and universal.[7] Every believer is responsible for exposing darkness and restoring the sinner, first personally, then corporately. The goal is always restoration to the body.

From time to time we hear pastors and leaders encouraging people to leave their church, or celebrating when some particularly difficult people leave. Sometimes they will spiritualize this by claiming God is "purifying" the church down to some remnant of faithful like Gideon's army. More truthfully, this masks a more sinister pleasure in disparaging or punishing fellow believers. Their purpose in confronting these believers was to motivate them to leave. This is neither reconciliation nor restoration. We must always confront in love, in order to restore.

Second, confrontation must be immediate. There is urgency in Scripture to go to the sinner directly and quickly, as soon as the sin is known. This urgency is founded upon the known danger and damaging impact of sin. The longer the sinner remains in darkness, the more resistant he is to light. Matthew 5 and 18 warn against waiting. If we are the sinner, we do not wait to see if anyone notices or takes offense. We are to go as soon as God makes us aware of our sin. Likewise, we do not wait for the sinner to realize his fault. We are to go and "show," or expose to the sinner his sin. Delay always brings more harm to the sinner and to the church because it allows both to remain in darkness.

Third, confronting sin is a prerequisite for, and must precede, worship. Matthew 5:23–24 and 1 Corinthians 1:17–34 warn those who would attempt to worship God falsely. True worshipers are those who "worship in spirit and in truth" (John 4:24). It is deceitful to come to worship or partake of the Communion bread and cup without confronting or confessing known sin. Worship must always be in the light. (The rise in tension between contemporary and traditional worship styles in many churches may be more of a symptom than a cause of church conflict.) So, Matthew 5:23 instructs the sinner to leave his gift at the altar and go be reconciled prior to worship.

In Genesis we read how God confronted Cain about his gift of worship.

> In the course of time Cain brought some of the fruits of the soil as an offering to the Lord. But Abel brought fat portions from some of the firstborn of his flock. The LORD looked with favor on Abel and his offering, but on Cain and his offering he did not look with favor. So Cain was very angry, and his face was downcast. Then the Lord said to Cain, "Why are you angry? Why is your face downcast? If you do what is right, will you not be accepted? But if you do not do what is right, sin is crouching at your door; it desires to have you, but you must master it." (Genesis 4:3–7)

This story goes against our notion of fairness. Cain offered his best, yet it was unacceptable. Who knew God would require blood?

"It is not fair," we hear Cain say, feeling sympathy for his case. It would help us to pause here and consider why we identify with Cain. As long as our focus is on Cain's predicament, we miss God's purpose. This story is not about Cain; it is about worship. Worship is never about us. Worship is always about God. As Elmer Towns has observed, "The first murder took place between brothers in disagreement over worship,"[8] and we have been fighting ever since. We cannot worship the Lord rightly if we are not living under His lordship and into His light.

CONFRONTING IN LOVE

To live into the light we must lovingly confront. This means going personally and lovingly to a brother or sister whenever a sin becomes known. When Peter was being duplicitous about Jewish and Gentile customs, the apostle Paul confronted him personally (to his face) and publicly (Galatians 2:11–14). Similarly, throughout the Epistles (notably in Hebrews) the writers at times combine bitter sarcasm with loving correction to shake the sinner into reality. This requires a boldness and a love that is uncommon and uncomfortable to most leaders.

Once, we were facilitating a meeting between church elders and a youth pastor who had just failed morally. One elder had previously spent a great deal of time and energy trying to help the young man. When the youth pastor confessed his sin to the elders, the elder who knew him best responded with frustration and passion. "How could you do this," he exclaimed, "after all the time we spent talking about these issues!" The youth pastor was taken aback, as were many of the other elders, who felt the elder was being too harsh.

But that elder was not being harsh; he was confronting the youth pastor, who had not fully understood the gravity of his sin. The confrontation was very direct, yet loving.

After airing emotions and stating consequences, the same elder looked the youth pastor in the eye and said, "Look at me. We love you, and we are going to get you through this. We are here to help you learn and grow through this." During the next weeks and months the elders came alongside the youth pastor to find counseling and personal support. The one elder called the youth pastor frequently to talk to him, encourage him, and hold him accountable.

This is a picture of biblical confrontation. Sin is sin and must be confronted. Love requires saying hard words in very direct ways.

Most believers are very reluctant to confront a brother or sister for fear of hurting the person or appearing judgmental. Fears of what the sinner will think or do often keep us from being obedient. Here, again, we are reminded that confrontation is not about us, neither the one confronting nor the one confronted, but about our collective life under the lordship of Christ.

Therefore, when you are called upon to confront, it is important to remember your role and responsibility under Christ:

1. You are responsible for speaking the truth in love and for being gentle, humble, and redemptive.

2. You are not responsible for the sinner's response.

3. You are not responsible for justice or vindication. These belong to God alone.

4. You can be confident that God's truth will prevail in His time. Nothing can thwart His purpose.

Confrontation requires a loving community, intentional teaching, and leaders who will model redemptive confrontation.

BECOMING ACCOUNTABLE

This begs certain questions for leaders: How are you held accountable? If sin is crouching unseen by you at your door, do others have your permission to warn you? If there is an issue in your life needing correction, is there a clear pathway for others to confront you?

If you do not have accountability, you are setting yourself and your church up for major failure. God did not intend you to work through your problems alone. He has called you into the body of Christ to be ministered to as well as to minister. One way to become accountable is to participate in a "Safe Place" group, which is discussed in the next section. However you do it, make confrontation and accountability a regular practice in your leadership.

LEADERS WHO MODEL LOVING CONFRONTATION

The best way to encourage loving confrontation in your church is to model it first in your church leadership. A simple principle of leadership is that leaders should never ask of their membership what they are unwilling to do themselves.

We recommend that you establish regular meetings with your

leadership team for confession, support, and mutual accountability.

Every church should establish accountability groups in the church to deal with conflict and sin, starting with leadership. Such groups provide a place of spiritual growth through truthful examination and loving confrontation over many years.

The purpose of an accountability group is for people to move into the light as men and women pursue and fulfill God's will in Christ for their lives under the authority of Scripture, the Holy Spirit, and God's work in this community of believers.

As the group grows in trust for one another, members should take more risks and speak to each other more directly as the Spirit reveals issues and concerns in their lives. The basis for this must always be Scripture guided by God's Spirit, not human opinions.

To speak Scripture into our lives there must be a sacred space. One accountability group structure, called the "Safe Place Group," includes the following elements: (1) prayer, (2) check-in, (3) repentance, (4) work, (5) intervention, (6) submission in trust, (6) accountability, (7) speaking into a person's life, and (8) contributing to the group.[9] For specifics on how this can work in your church, see the appendix, "Forming a Safe Place Group."

Recently, we have implemented and recommended a similar curriculum, called Life Transformation Groups.[10] The groups consist of no more than three people, men with men and women with women, who do three things. First, they meet weekly for regular confession, asking accountability questions of one another. Second, they commit to reading large portions of Scripture prior to coming together. When they gather, each member asks the others, "How has God spoken through His Word this week?" The third component is intentional prayer for the lost.

When confrontation is an ongoing commitment, learned in small groups and practiced in the wider body, the church moves collectively into the light.

Biblical Guidelines for Confrontation

Every church should have biblical guidelines for confronting sin redemptively. The following are steps Jesus outlines for the church. Except for step six, all come from the gospel of Matthew.

1. Upon discovery of sin in your life or the life of a fellow believer, go promptly and lovingly confess or confront the fellow believer in private (5:23; 18:15).

2. If the fellow believer listens and renounces sin, grant forgiveness in Jesus' name (18:15, 21–35).

3. If the sinner refuses to listen, return to admonish the believer again in the presence of one or two witnesses (18:16).

4. If the sinner still refuses to listen, the matter should be brought before your church leaders (18:17). The leaders should investigate the matter carefully and thoroughly, discussing the specific charges with the believer.

5. If there is no evidence of repentance, or if the believer refuses to cooperate in the process, the church body should be made aware of sin (18:17).

6. If there is still no evidence of repentance, fellowship with this believer should be broken until there is repentance (2 Thessalonians 3:6, 14; 1 Corinthians 5:11; Titus 3:10–11).

7. God gives the church authority to "bind" and "loose," to withhold fellowship and to forgive (18:18).

How to Lead a Confrontation

On occasion, leaders will be called upon to intervene in a dispute between unreconciled members, or to confront a sinner who is unrepentant. When this occurs, the following guidelines should be followed:

1. Pray. Thank God for what He is going to reveal and do in and through the meeting. Ask the Spirit of Truth to be present; call upon God's wisdom, grace, and mercy to guide the meeting.

2 Explain the goal of reconciliation. Explain how and why all are there: to seek reconciliation. Be sure to introduce those who do not know one another, and then briefly explain the role and function of each person. Remind participants that they are not here together so that one will win and another lose, or that one is right and another wrong. The goal, rather, is reconciliation. God's righteousness is to be worked out over time in every area of everyone's life, specifically in this conflict.

3. Accept the lordship of Jesus Christ. Remind all that we gather in Jesus' name, on the basis of His life, death, and resurrection. Therefore, all participants are loved, respected, and valued. Affirm our mutual submission to the lordship of Christ and to God's desire for reconciliation. Be positive, stating that we have an opportunity to listen and discern God's voice through one another.

4. Enter into the light. Define current reality by exposing sin and stating clearly, specifically, and objectively the exact nature of the conflict or problem. Present facts as they are known, not personal opinion. (If the injured party is present, ask him or her to state in first-person terms how he was hurt or offended, and to confess and ask forgiveness where he was wrong.)

5. Submit to God's truth. Invite all present to submit their lives and thoughts before God's Word. Introduce Scripture as a standard to follow and to understand more. Use Scripture to build up, not to tear down (Ephesians 4:29). Read a passage from the Bible. Do not quote a verse as proof without context, or "preach." If possible, have the person read the passage; then ask, "What would obedience to this passage mean?"

6. Describe the nature of the problem and what proper obedience would be. First, describe the problem—what it looks like from

the facts presented. Ask the person if the charge or facts as presented are understood, or are they confused. Is there something wrong or missing that needs to be stated? Ask each person what he/she understands the conflict or problem to be. Second, ask each person to describe what it would look like to follow Jesus through this conflict or problem.

7. Discuss viewpoints. Invite response and discussion. Allow differing descriptions. Allow silence. Do not interrupt, and do not debate or rush to conclusions. Validate feelings and concerns without endorsing behavior or supporting conclusions. To properly understand the viewpoints and issues, ask clarifying questions, such as, "Are you saying . . ?"; "Tell me more about . . . Can you give me an example of . . ."; "I'm confused about . . ." Be sure to restate or paraphrase their concerns to be sure you have them right. For instance, begin your response with: "The way you see it, then, is . . ."; "From your perspective, I was wrong to say . . ."; or "It sounds like you were hurt when . . ."

8. Discern God's voice and will. Summarize the differences and agreements between the parties. Ask each person to consider what it would mean for him, personally, to submit to the Holy Spirit and to each other "in the Lord." In light of what God is saying through the group, what is best? (It might be appropriate to stop and pray.) Here the facilitator may need to exercise discernment by warning, correcting, or rebuking attitudes or behaviors that are resisting grace. This does not mean taking a side or favoring an opinion in the dispute, but rather, encouraging faith and mutual submission.

9. Decide to act. Ask each participant what he/she is prepared to do. Offer solutions prepared beforehand, modifying as needed by what was learned. If confession is made and forgiveness given, agree on what, if any, public or private restitution needs to be made. Agree on a commitment to not dwell on or bring up the incident further. If reconciliation is resisted, ask what is missing or what would be necessary for him/her to be reconciled. If

the participant refuses, warn that refusing reconciliation is a greater issue than the presenting problem. It is an offense against the Cross and unacceptable in the church.

10. Commit to act. Inform and agree upon specific next steps for confession, reconciliation, and restitution.

11. Pray. End the meeting with prayer. Thank God for grace and forgiveness made possible through the life, death, and resurrection of Jesus Christ.

Living into the light requires personal examination and corporate confrontation. The initiative is always with you (personal and singular).

When believers refuse to examine or receive confrontation, the church leadership must intervene. The goal is never to prosecute or defend. Rather, the leader's task is always to invite believers into a process of reconciliation marked by humility and submission.

Leaders must always frame the conversation and actions as an invitation to accept and practice the principles of peace made possible by Jesus Christ. Ultimately, leaders invite the sinner and the one sinned against into a way of life shaped by the Cross.

Notes

1. Geoffrey Bromiley, ed., *Theological Dictionary of the New Testament* (Grand Rapids: Eerdmans, 1985), 40.
2. Ibid., 8–9.
3. See Genesis 6:5; Jeremiah 17:9.
4. 1 Corinthians 6.
5. I first heard this question, or one like it, in conversation with Martin Sanders, associate professor of preaching at Alliance Theological Seminary in Nyack, N.Y.
6. See also Nehemiah 9:17, 29; Jeremiah 7:26; 17:23; 19:15; Acts 7:51.
7. John Howard Yoder, "Binding and Loosing," *The Royal Priesthood* (Scottdale, Pa.: Herald, 1998), 325–37.
8. Elmer Towns, *Putting an End to Worship Wars* (Nashville: Broadman & Holman, 1997), 47.
9. The term *Safe Place* and the sequence have been adapted from mutual conversations and practice with my friend David Fitch, Ph.D.
10. Neil Cole, *Cultivating a Life for God* (St. Charles, Ill.: ChurchSmart Resources, 1999),

Twelve

CONFESSION AND FORGIVENESS:
HOW WE MUST RESPOND

*Therefore confess your sins to each other and pray for
each other so that you may be healed.*

∽ JAMES 5:16

Joe had been the "church boss" for more than thirty years, outlasting many pastors. He was a good man who wanted the best. But the best usually meant his way. So Joe was always on the church board and always on the pastor's case.

When Joe saw something wrong or disagreed with a decision, he'd write a letter, a very long letter with his "suggestions." He was relentless. Joe wore down and wore out eight different senior and associate pastors through three decades. When two pastors left the church one recent spring, the denomination leader called Metanoia Ministries to see if we could help the church.

In the past, many attempts had been made by pastors and elders to confront Joe. A year earlier the church had called in a Christian conciliation group for mediation. But nothing changed because only the interpersonal, not the systemic, issues were addressed.

When the problem resurfaced, Joe was asked to resign his church membership or face disciplinary action. He left the church but refused to resign his membership or to stop his protest.

I listened to the denomination leader describe the problem. "We can help with the discipline," I said, "but the problem in the church is more complex than one difficult man." The church had learned to accept and even enable his dysfunction. This had to be confronted also.

Church conflict is always systemic, never simple; usually far more theological than interpersonal. When church leaders look only at events and interpersonal concerns, they address the symptoms, not the cause. Like snapping the flower off a dandelion on a spring lawn, the yellow goes away but the weed actually grows as the roots sink deeper. The next fall and spring you have bigger, stronger weeds.

The same principle applies to the church: When leaders try to encourage faith without correcting bad theology or rebuking sin, the problem grows bigger and deeper.

The problem in Joe's church involved the whole church. We suggested a church assessment. That is how three men and two women—all trained by Metanoia—came to spend four days interviewing most members of Joe's church.

Meanwhile, my first day at the church included a two-hour meeting with Joe. He talked for ninety minutes about his role in the church history, measuring time by clicking off each senior or associate pastor's weakness and why each had to leave.

I listened, noting patterns. Then I asked Joe about his role—how he may have contributed to the problem. "You are good at naming the weaknesses of others," I suggested, "but what are your weaknesses, Joe?"

Joe responded in a way that is typical of critical and controlling personalities; he defined himself by what he is not. "I am not a passive person," he said. "I'm not afraid to challenge people. . . . I don't believe in being a dictator. . . . I don't have to have the last word."

All his descriptions were negative assertions. When I pointed this out, Joe could not see it.

"You said you are not passive, Joe," I replied. "I doubt if anyone in the church thinks you are! The question is, are you aggressive?"

"I suppose I can be a bit harsh at times," Joe admitted. This was the most ownership Joe would take.

"Either this church has extraordinarily bad 'luck' in choosing pastors," I suggested, "or there is another factor—one that has stayed on after each pastor left. There is one constancy in your stories, Joe," I said. "You. What do you attribute this to?"

Joe was defensive, but he knew I was listening to him and that I respected him. In fact, I agreed with many of Joe's concerns about the church and told him so. "God has given you wisdom and discernment," I said, "but you are arguing for the right causes in all the wrong ways. People can't hear what you are saying because of how you are saying it."

Joe agreed to meet with me again at the end of all the interviews. I asked him to spend the next two days humbly asking the Lord to show him where he had been wrong—"to own your part in the problem."

CONFRONTING A CONTROLLING AND CRITICAL SPIRIT

In the meantime, our assessment uncovered many weaknesses and issues in the church that members and leaders alike needed to address. But Joe was at the center of every conflict. We had to confront Joe for his prideful, controlling, and critical spirit.

We often have to patiently and carefully "correct, rebuke and encourage" (2 Timothy 4:2). The apostle Paul instructed Timothy to rebuke sin, correct bad theology or thinking, and encourage faith. This is the stuff of biblical leadership and reconciliation.

In most instances, these confrontations are with leaders—pastors, elders, and deacons. The range of issues is wide, from the sensational to the subtle. For instance, at Metanoia, during the past year we confronted sins of adultery, homosexuality, pornography, divorce/separation, mistreatment of women, abuse of authority, addictive behavior, satanic ritual abuse, and false teaching. We have also confronted sins of stealing, lying, threatening to sue, tax evasion, quitting, manipulation, slander, failure to shepherd, lack of submission, gossip, and anger.

It would be debilitating to deal with these issues were it not for the grace and mercy of God to change minds and hearts. Some leaders choose not to be reconciled, and we mourn for them. But many others respond with humility and brokenness, pointing to the power of the Cross to redeem and restore.

The assessment team met with Joe and his wife on Saturday night. We asked Joe how God had spoken to him in the past two days. Joe started out defensively, retelling how he had been hurt by others. We acknowledged that others had failed and sinned against Joe. "But we are meeting with you now, Joe, not them," I said. "We are here to help you discover and reconcile what you did wrong."

TWO OPTIONS

We talked with Joe for two hours, listening to him and pointing out the evidence of his failure. It was clear God had begun to break Joe of his pride and control. We explained that he was at a crossroads with two options before him. He could humble himself, own his sin publicly before the congregation, and submit to a process of restitution, or he could continue to insist on his being right and refusing reconciliation.

If he chose to humble himself, we told him that his legacy at the church would be one of humility and grace. If he chose the present path he was on, we would recommend the church proceed to discipline, and he would likely be forced to leave the church in dishonor and disgrace.

"The bottom line is this, Joe," I said. "Do you want to be 'right' or do you want to be reconciled?"

Joe chose reconciliation. We asked him to make a public confession and to submit to a process that would reconstitute his character—to place himself under the elders. Joe agreed.

He met with the elders before the service the following day. Joe told us he had not slept much the night before. "I did not really fully understand what you were saying to me," Joe said, "until late into the night." God convicted Joe of his arrogance, and he began to see what others had been trying to tell him for years—that God must be in control, God must receive the glory. "I see it all so clearly now," Joe said.

At a meeting that afternoon, we gave our report, calling the church to a time of repentance and renewal. When we announced the findings of sin, I read a public rebuke about Joe that cited how he had hurt many people and harmed the church by his critical spirit and controlling attitude. (I had read and discussed the statement personally with Joe beforehand.)

A HUMBLE RESPONSE

Joe came to the lectern to make his confession.

With tears and brokenness, Joe humbled himself before the congregation, fully acknowledging his sin and the hurt he had caused many in the church. He apologized to his wife and family also, who embraced him in tears at the front of the church.

"It is our great privilege and responsibility," I said following Joe's confession, "to grant forgiveness in Jesus' name. Joe has acknowledged the hurt of his sin and has asked you for forgiveness. I invite several of you to represent the congregation in proclaiming public forgiveness to Joe."

The first man to stand was a leader who had served with and had been hurt by Joe several years earlier during an especially difficult time in the church. "Speaking for myself and on behalf of the church," he said, "we forgive you, Joe." Several people stood and spoke words of love and forgiveness to Joe and to his family. God's peace and joy rested on this family and on the church.

Before the service was over I instructed the congregation that because of the power of forgiveness, these matters were over. I explained that Joe would be meeting with the elders to make restitution, but the matters confessed and forgiven no longer existed.

"Let me warn you," I said, "if any person ever attempts to bring these matters up again, that person will be sinning against Joe, against this church, and against the blood of Jesus Christ. These matters are closed."

THE POWER OF CONFESSION

In the previous chapter we considered how living into the light requires personal examination and corporate confrontation. These, in turn, require a response. Once we're aware of our sin, we must confess.

We frequently receive calls from denominations asking for advice about how to manage a leader's sin. Our response is to say, "You don't manage sin, you renounce it."

"But this issue will split the church [or "hurt people" or "ruin a reputation"]," they say, "if the sin becomes public knowledge."

Our experience is that practicing redemption is always less painful to the church and always more helpful to the sinner. When sin is confessed openly, humbly, and completely as soon as it becomes known, the sinner and community can embody reconciliation. Silence and cover-up, on the other hand, invite heaviness and harm. Solomon counseled, "He who conceals his sins does not prosper, but whoever confesses and renounces them finds mercy" (Proverbs 28:13).

Witness David's words in Psalm 32:2–5:

Blessed is the man whose sin the Lord does not count against him and in whose spirit is no deceit. When I kept silent, my bones wasted away through my groaning all day long. For day and night your hand was heavy upon me; my strength was sapped as in the heat of summer. Then I acknowledged my sin to you and did not cover up my iniquity. I said, "I will confess my transgressions to the LORD"—and you forgave the guilt of my sin.

The great Scottish writer George MacDonald once wrote "Our sins are crimes that will hunt us, either to the bosom of God or to the pit of hell."[1]

When a pastor or Christian leader falls, the first—and worst—possible reaction is to cover up. It is always wrong. First and foremost, it is wrong because Scripture says it is. Confession was, from early on, the primary means for Israel to make themselves right with God (Leviticus 5:5). In the New Testament, confession was (and is) the means by which men and women found salvation and sanctification. "If you confess with your mouth, 'Jesus is Lord,' and believe in your heart that God raised him from the dead, you will be saved" (Romans 10:9).

With confession always comes forgiveness—forgiveness by God. The apostle John wrote, "If we confess our sins, he is faithful and just and will forgive us our sins and purify us from all unrighteousness" (1 John 1:9).

We must note again that these verses were written to the church, to believers. Confession is not a one-time event for unbelievers but a continual practice for the church, a way of life. Confession is the very means for growing and forming our character, changing our habits, and renewing our mind. The apostle James even hints that our health is dependent upon regular confession. "Confess your sins to each other and pray for each other so that you may be healed" (James 5:16). Unconfessed sin, the context of this passage suggests, leads to trouble and sickness.

Why Don't We Confess?

So why don't we confess? I suspect that here, as in so many other places, we adopt the habits of our culture rather than apply the values of the Cross. The assumption of our culture is that people are good and that sin is private. If people are good and sin is private, then we need acceptance, not forgiveness; a therapist, not community. Theologian L. Gregory Jones writes, "The rise of therapy cannot be understood without simultaneously recognizing both the complicity of the church and its failure to embody practices of love, forgiveness and reconciliation."[2]

It is a telling, shameful sign of our syncretism that the church would rather refer a sinner to an outside expert to handle his "private" pathologies than apply the power of the Cross through corporate confession and forgiveness.

If the church is to be the church, redemption must be taught and modeled by leaders. It has always been so. Consider Moses, David, and Peter. Each committed significant sins while they were leaders. The very fact that these sins are recorded in Scripture tells us how God views the public disclosure of sin. If the church is the body of Christ and we (all believers) are members of it, then there is no right to privacy. There is no private sin. All sin belongs to the church.

What should surprise us, then, is not that Christian leaders sin—we are sinners—but that we do not put into practice the distinguishing characteristic of our redemptive story—confession. Instead, we cover up.

Church conflict grows to the extent that confession is ignored. If the church is to be the church, we must recover the lost art of biblical confession. Leadership must model and mentor confessional community.

A Definition of Confession

The New Testament uses two Greek words for "confession." The first word is *homologeo,* which adds the prefix *homo,* meaning "the same as" to the root word *logos,* meaning "word." This word for confession literally means "saying the same words." To confess is to so agree with God and others about a matter that we would use the very same words that they would use to describe it. In the context of sin, we would agree by restating the charge against us.

The second word used in Scripture is *exologeo,* which adds the prefix *ex,* meaning "out of," to *logos.* Here, confession means to profess, "to speak out," to bear testimony to the truth of the Gospel. Confession is the public declaration that Jesus is Lord through a public thanksgiving for salvation or a public ownership of sin.

Confession is the gateway to embodying the Gospel story. Acknowledging sin is the first step to declaring the lordship of Christ and entering into a way of life shaped by the Cross.

When leaders fail to confess, they disobey Scripture, and they violate the trust of their people—making two problems when there was once only one. The second problem—the failure to confess— is the greater problem because it denies the power and reality of the Cross.

Our experience working with fallen leaders follows the same pattern of Scripture. When a leader confesses sin specifically and completely, submitting to a process of transformation, that leader is broken and healed; often he is restored to greater ministry. When a leader refuses to confess or submit, that leader always grows distant and bitter. Frequently that leader ends up destroying (often by self-sabotage) his marriage and his ministry.

CONFESSION AND COMMUNITY

Confession forces you to agree with God about your sin. In confession you see yourself as you are—desperately in need of a Savior. Confession with "one another" rehearses that condition with a brother and a sister. Together you "agree" in your common need for Jesus Christ.

Likewise, prayer acknowledges your condition before God and

in front of your brother or sister. Together, you acknowledge that God alone, not man or methods, is sufficient to make you "whole." Prayer restores your relationship with God and with your brothers and sisters. Through prayer we become one. We become a true community.

In his classic book *Life Together,* Dietrich Bonhoeffer described how sin works to separate us from fellowship.

> *He who is alone with his sin is utterly alone. It may be that Christians, notwithstanding corporate worship, common prayer, and all their fellowship in service, may still be left to their loneliness. The final breakthrough to fellowship does not occur, because, though they have fellowship with one another as believers and as devout people, they do not have fellowship as the undevout, as sinners. The pious fellowship permits no one to be a sinner. So everybody must conceal his sin from himself and from the fellowship. We dare not be sinners. Many Christians are unthinkably horrified when a real sinner is suddenly discovered among the righteous. So we remain alone with our sin, living in lies and hypocrisy. The fact is we are sinners![3]*

For Bonhoeffer, the solution to our loneliness was to admit that we are sinners through confession.

> *In confession the breakthrough to community takes place. Sin demands to have a man by himself. It withdraws him from the community. The more isolated a person is, the more destructive will be the power of sin over him, and the more deeply he becomes involved in it, the more disastrous is his isolation. Sin wants to remain unknown. In confession the light of the Gospel breaks into the darkness and seclusion of the heart. The sin must be brought into the light. The unexpressed must be openly spoken and acknowledged. All that is secret and hidden is manifest. . . . Since the confession of sin is made in the presence of a Christian brother, the last stronghold of self-justification is abandoned. The sinner surrenders. . . . He gives up his heart to God and he finds forgiveness of all sin in the*

fellowship of Jesus Christ and his brother. . . . Now he stands in the fellowship of sinners who live by the grace of God in the Cross of Jesus Christ.[4]

Many decades have passed since Bonhoeffer wrote these words, but they are as timely for the church now as in his day.

A CALL FOR CONFESSION IN THE CHURCH

We need to recover confession in the church for at least three reasons: (1) to glorify God, (2) to form personal character, and (3) to build the community of believers. Let's look at how confession achieves all three outcomes.

CONFESSION IS GOD-GLORIFYING

We need to recover confession in the church first of all because it glorifies Jesus Christ. When believers stand and admit failure or bear testimony to the power of the Cross in their lives, Jesus is declared Lord and His name is honored. Jesus Himself gave us a model of such testimony when, full of joy through the Holy Spirit, he said, "I praise you, Father, Lord of heaven and earth, because you have hidden these things from the wise and learned, and revealed them to little children. Yes, Father, for this was your good pleasure" (Luke 10:21). To confess is to acknowledge who God is and what He has done.

Confession is the response of the heart in faith before God. In the Gospels we frequently hear this confession in response to uncertainty. Jesus asked His disciples who they said He was, and Peter proclaimed, "You are the Christ, the Son of the living God" (Matthew 16:16).

When Jesus met Martha after Lazarus' death, He said, "I am the resurrection and the life. He who believes in me will live, even though he dies; and whoever lives and believes in me will never die. Do you believe this?"

Martha responded, "Yes, Lord, I believe that you are the Christ, the Son of God, who was to come into the world" (John 11: 25–27).

And one day, Scripture notes, "every knee [will] bow . . . and every tongue confess that Jesus Christ is Lord, to the glory of God the Father" (Philippians 2:10–11). Confession is God-glorifying.

CONFESSION IS CHARACTER-FORMING

Confession forms character. The act of confession is the first step in a commitment to change. When a believer confesses any struggle or sin—whether it be an addiction to alcohol or drugs, moral failure, or simply admitting that "I don't know how to handle my kids" or "I don't know what to do with my anger toward my wife"— the mere act of confession emboldens a believer to change. Confession is a public commitment to turn around and go another way. It is a declaration of determination to change with a request for help.

This commitment is, itself, character-forming. In confession, the sinner makes a commitment to the Lord and to the church to walk a new path. This is why discipline and restitution are vital steps for reconciliation. A confession is the start of a transformation process. As brothers and sisters gather around to forgive, to guide, and to hold accountable, habits of thinking and behaving are changed; character is reconstituted and formed anew. There is no quick fix to forming character. It takes time, prayer, and a commitment to work out salvation together.

God has given all believers everything we need for godliness. He has given us His Word, which is powerful, effective, and life-giving. He has given us His Holy Spirit, who is able to convict and empower. He has given us the body of Christ to hear our confessions and come alongside in support. Confession welcomes all three into our character formation.

CONFESSION IS COMMUNITY-BUILDING

Finally, confession builds community. When the members of a local church submit and confess in mutuality under the lordship of Jesus Christ, a bond of unity, trust, and love is formed and the body is built up. As we're confessing—speaking the truth in love— "we will in all things grow up into him who is the Head, that is, Christ" (Ephesians 4:15).

Confession reminds us of our common life, our communion, together. That is why the Scripture warns against coming to the Communion table with unconfessed sin. As Bonhoeffer wrote:

> The fellowship of the Lord's Supper is the superlative fulfillment of Christian fellowship. As the members of the congregation are united in body and blood at the table of the Lord so will they be together in eternity. Here the community has reached its goal. Here joy in Christ and his community is complete. The life of Christians together under the Word has reached its perfection in the sacrament.[5]

Confession is modeled best as leaders take responsibility for their faults, their failures, and their sins in a way that is consistent and sensitive to the body of Christ that they're serving.

All conflict is ultimately about leadership—how leaders respond to conflict and how they acknowledge their faults. Leaders must make public confessions because they are sinners, they are part of the community, and they provide an example to follow. The leader who confesses sin joins the community of sinners who proclaim faith in Christ alone, not man or method, as the object of worship. Meeting one another at the foot of the cross, leaders and members alike look up to Christ.

A church will not grow beyond the example of its leaders. The manner and method of how leaders lead will be mirrored in the life of the church. If leaders do not confess, neither will their people. A leader who will not confess has no authority to confront or discipline sin in the congregation. Leaders must confess because they're sinners, they live in community, and they are an example to others.

How to Make a Public Confession

There are five simple steps to making a public confession.

First, the confessor must own the problem specifically. A confession is a specific statement of what was thought, said, or practiced. A confession is unconditional. Confession names the sin and addresses the circumstances directly—agreeing with God and all those offended that the sinner is wrong.

Second, the sinner must confess the sin completely. By completely we mean without qualification and stating all of the sin involved.

The sinner states clearly, "When I did or thought or said this, it was wrong. I am agreeing with God and others that I was wrong." Confession means there are "no ifs, ands, or buts." Many confessions offered in public life are not confessions; they are pleas for amnesty. A confession is not, "If I've hurt anyone," or "If I've offended anyone, I'm sorry." A confession is, "I did this, and I am grieved in my heart. I am convicted by God that I did it, and I apologize. I own it completely. I was wrong."

Neither should anyone confess partial wrong, knowing there is more to be said that, as yet, has not been found out. Leaders must be very careful to explore the full extent of the sin before inviting a sinner to confess. Great harm comes to the church when a sinner confesses and is forgiven for a sin, only to find out that the circumstances and events were much greater than admitted. This is particularly true of addictive behaviors and moral failure. Adultery is quite often associated with pornography. The longer the practice of sin, the greater likelihood that other sins are present. The person must confess *all* the sin. Confession must be complete so that forgiveness, restitution, and restoration may be final.

Third, once a sinner has confessed specifically and completely, the sinner must ask for forgiveness humbly. "I recognize that my sin caused hurt and harm to God, to others, to myself. I am wrong. Please forgive me." Sin is costly and damaging. Darkness wants us to minimize the impact our words and behavior have on ourselves and others.

All sin is harmful to the church in direct and indirect ways. The sinner must acknowledge the harm done. Gossip is a crime against the church body, not merely the person talked about. Adultery is a sin against the church, not merely the spouse and family. The sins of adults are sins against the teenagers and children who look on in silent witness.

Fourth, the sinner should state a commitment to turn around and, when circumstances warrant, ask the body for help to change. "I want to change, and I ask for your prayer and for your accountability."

After this, the sinner should sit down and shut up. A confession is short, to the point, and heartfelt. It offers no explanation or excuse. It is not the time to describe what has been learned or how God has healed you. Own the problem, ask for forgiveness, then sit down and be quiet.

Fifth, the sinner should begin to make restitution immediately. Let repentance demonstrate your "good confession" through a changed mind and changed behavior.[6]

WHAT CINDY LEARNED

As the pastor was completing his sermon, Cindy could take it no longer. She stood up from her chair and interrupted the pastor mid-sentence, accusing him of deceit, while five hundred congregants sat in stunned silence. Everyone was shocked. The elders did not know what to say or do. The pastor fumbled through the rest of the sermon, and the service ended abruptly.

We heard about Cindy's actions about six months later when we conducted an assessment in her church. When we asked interviewees when they had been most embarrassed or frustrated in the church, almost every person recalled the incident with Cindy. When I interviewed Cindy I asked her about it. She admitted that she was wrong and said she went to the pastor to apologize and ask forgiveness immediately. The pastor granted forgiveness, and Cindy felt the problem was over.

"Not quite," I responded. I explained how Cindy's sin was not only an affront against the pastor and his authority but against the whole church. Cindy understood and asked what she should do. "You need to make a public confession," I advised, "because your sin was a public sin." Cindy understood.

"You are right, I need to do that," she said. I encouraged Cindy to write out her confession.

The next Saturday night, I got a call from Cindy. "Jim, I've taken your advice," she said. "I'm going to make a public confession. I'd like to read it to you." She did, but her confession did much more than confess; she declared how her mistake had helped the church to grow and taught her wonderful lessons during the past six months.

I commended her humble acknowledgment of her sin—the first three sentences of the "confession"—and then said the rest had to go. Cindy was taken aback by my assessment.

"Really? It took me several days to write this, because I wanted to share with the people what I've learned."

"No, Cindy," I said. "You are the sinner. You have no authority or integrity to tell the people what you've learned. You've not earned the right to teach them anything. You have sinned against these people. You need forgiveness." I went on to explain that if God wanted her to share what she had learned, the best way to do that would be by her life, not her words.

"You are accountable to own your sin, to take responsibility for the hurt and dissension it caused, and to ask for forgiveness," I said. "Then you need to sit down and be quiet. Perhaps, in time, there will be an appropriate time for you to share what God has done in your life. But not now."

We talked some more, and just before ending the call I asked, "By the way, how are you planning to make the confession?"

"Well, I thought I'd just stand up like I did the first time," Cindy said.

"No, you're not going to do that," I replied. "Here's what should happen. At the end of the service, the pastor needs to recognize you and welcome you to the pulpit. Your sin was against the authority of the pulpit, as well as the pastor and church. The congregation must know that you are under the pastor's authority and have his permission in making this confession."

At the end of the service the next morning, Cindy made her confession. The pastor had read and approved the statement Cindy was to make. He said, "Cindy has a word to say. She has my permission to say it. I'm asking her to come forward." Cindy made her simple but profound confession, and the church granted forgiveness in Jesus' name.

THE RESPONSE OF FORGIVENESS

The Greek word for *forgive* literally means "to give graciously; to give freely." Biblical forgiveness cannot be understood outside of God's grace and love. In fact, God invites our participation in His grace through forgiveness.

In thousands of churches each week, millions of believers pray these simple, profound words: "Forgive us our debts, as we also have forgiven our debtors" (Matthew 6:12). We pray the Lord's Prayer because Jesus taught His disciples to pray this way. But we often forget why or the implications of our words. Jesus explained, "For if you forgive men when they sin against you, your heavenly Father will also forgive you. But if you do not forgive men their sins, your Father will not forgive your sins" (Matthew 6:14–15).

This teaching ought to terrify us. Jesus is saying that our forgiveness from God is proportionate to our willingness to forgive others. How are you doing with forgiveness? The plain truth is this: If you are refusing to forgive others, God is refusing to forgive you.

"Then Peter came to Jesus and asked, 'Lord, how many times

shall I forgive my brother when he sins against me? Up to seven times?' Jesus answered, 'I tell you, not seven times, but seventy-seven times'" (Matthew 18:21–22).

The Pharisees taught that a man should forgive an offense up to three times. Peter, knowing this tradition, presented an option making him twice the benefactor. Jesus answered, in effect, "No, not seven times, but every time."

REMEMBERING WHAT WE HAVE RECEIVED

Jesus taught that to understand forgiveness we must remember what we have received. Forgiveness is always a gift. How can anyone who has given much, offer little in return?

To illustrate, Jesus told a parable about a servant who owed his master a sum the servant could not ever repay. When his master demanded payment, the servant fell at his master's feet. "Be patient with me," he begged, "and I will pay back everything." The master took pity on the servant and forgave him.

When this same servant found a fellow servant who owed him a payable sum, he grabbed and choked him. "Pay back what you owe me!" he demanded. The fellow servant fell to his knees and begged for mercy, but the servant refused. Instead he had the other servant thrown into prison "until he could pay the debt." (See Matthew 18:23–30.)

There is great irony in Jesus' story. The first servant owed a sum no amount of time or work could ever pay off, yet he asked for patience. He did not ask for the debt to be forgiven, but for the master to accept his lie that he would someday repay. Yet, the master forgave him completely. The wicked servant subsequently met a man who owed him a sum that could easily be repaid in a short time. Yet when the fellow servant promised to work off the debt, the wicked servant rejected the arrangement, throwing the man in jail.

Those listening to Jesus would have seen the injustice and irony immediately, and they would have resonated with how the parable ends—with the wicked servant being thrown into prison himself. But just as the listeners were nodding their heads in agreement, Jesus turned the parable on them (and on us), saying, "This is how my heavenly Father will treat each of you unless you forgive your brother from your heart" (Matthew 18:35).

At least two lessons must be drawn from the parable. First, forgiveness is a gift. Second, forgiveness is a response of the heart. Forgiveness reveals more about our relationship to God than our relationship to the sinner.

WHAT IT MEANS TO FORGIVE LIKE JESUS

Scripture tells us to forgive like Jesus: "Bear with each other and forgive whatever grievances you may have against one another. Forgive as the Lord forgave you" (Colossians 3:13). So, how did the Lord forgive us?

Earlier in Colossians, Paul wrote, "When you were dead in your sins and in the uncircumcision of your sinful nature, God made you alive with Christ. He forgave us all our sins, having canceled the written code, with its regulations, that was against us and that stood opposed to us; he took it away, nailing it to the cross" (2:13–14). God forgave us freely.

Forgiveness is never based upon the merit of the sinner. In fact, the sinner, like the wicked servant in the parable above, can never hope to earn forgiveness. The law tells us that we are utterly unworthy and completely depraved. Our guilt before God deserves punishment. God forgives the repentant sinner freely.

To forgive means to do so freely. It also means to do so no matter the cost. Indeed, Jesus' forgiveness was costly. The physical and spiritual pain He suffered to forgive our sins was described by the prophet Isaiah centuries before it happened. The Messiah was "familiar with suffering. . . . Pierced for our transgressions, he was crushed for our iniquities; the punishment that brought us peace was upon him, and by his wounds we are healed." By making "his life a guilt offering," Jesus brought salvation to sinners like you and me. As God declared, "By his knowledge my righteous servant will justify many, and he will bear their iniquities" (53:3, 5, 10–11). Read Isaiah 53:3–11 to catch the scope of suffering by this humble Servant.

Our forgiveness of others is founded upon the unmerited and costly gift Christ has given to us. The Gospel calls us to embody forgiveness, to live out personally and corporately the forgiveness that is ours in Jesus Christ—a forgiveness unmatched in the world and displayed in His death-sacrifice. That death—and Christ's resurrection victory over death—is the focus and the power of all forgiveness.

It is Christ, not our understanding or acceptance of events, that makes forgiveness possible.

How to Forgive Like Jesus

In our work with conflicted churches, we have ministered to men and women who have survived and perpetrated horrible crimes or acts of abuse. How does a believer forgive someone who rapes, abuses, or murders a loved one?

The only sufficient answer is in the Cross of Christ. No act of brutality, no offense we have suffered is greater than the price Jesus paid for our forgiveness. To refuse forgiveness when a sinner repents is simply not an option. We must forgive, or we deny the power of the Cross.

At times, when a sinner repents and the church forgives, we have to warn victims who refuse to forgive. The difficult message a leader must give is, "You will forgive, or you will not be a part of our body." There is no option not to forgive when the body of Christ grants forgiveness. Forgiveness does not forget the crime or minimize the hurt. Forgiveness looks to Christ, whose suffering on the cross bears our grief. Forgiveness is not an act of our will; it is submission to Christ's completed work. We cannot forgive alone, nor does God ask us to. Without the body of Christ we cannot forgive like Jesus. The church is the primary agent for reconciliation and place of forgiveness.[7]

This is what makes the Gospel so alarming: that there is room in our pews for rapists and murderers who repent, but no room for their victims who refuse to forgive. Why? Because refusing reconciliation is an affront to the Cross. It says, "My pain is greater than the sufficiency of Christ."

LOVE AND FORGIVENESS

Forgiveness is always linked to love; forgiveness is the power to love. Consider the account in Luke 7 of Jesus' dinner at a Pharisee's house. When "a woman who had lived a sinful life" appeared at the house, she opened an alabaster jar of perfume. "As she stood behind him at his feet weeping, she began to wet his feet with her tears. Then she wiped them with her hair, kissed them and poured perfume on them" (vv. 37–38). The Pharisee responded by thinking Jesus was merely a so-called prophet, unable to recognize the woman as a sinner. Jesus answered the man's thoughts with a parable illustrating that those who have greater debts forgiven will show greater love. Then, turning toward the woman, he told the Pharisee:

> "Do you see this woman? I came into your house. You did not give me any water for my feet, but she wet my feet with her tears and wiped them with her hair. You did not give me a kiss, but this woman, from the time I entered, has not stopped kissing my feet. You did not put oil on my head, but she has poured perfume on my feet. Therefore, I tell you, her many sins have been forgiven—for she loved much. But he who has been forgiven little loves little." Then Jesus said to her, "Your sins are forgiven." (Luke 7:44–48)

The woman washing Jesus' feet demonstrated her outpouring love for the Lord. Then Jesus connected love to forgiveness: "I tell you, her many sins have been forgiven—for she loved much." To emphasize the point, Jesus continued, "But he who has been forgiven little loves little."

Here again Jesus spoke of forgiveness in reciprocal terms. Love follows forgiveness. Those who have been forgiven much love much; those forgiven little, love little. Those who refuse forgiveness refuse the love of Christ.

FORGIVENESS AND PHARISAISM

Forgiveness is the power to free the sinner from sin and the church from legalism. The Pharisees saw sin as a matter of punishing the sinner and proving right and wrong. Jesus saw forgiveness as the power of light over darkness.

When a woman caught in adultery was brought before Jesus to be stoned, Jesus answered the crowd by saying that the one without sin should be the first to cast a stone. When the crowd dispersed, Jesus asked the woman, "'Where are they? Has no one condemned you?' 'No one, sir,' she said. 'Then neither do I condemn you,' Jesus declared. 'Go now, and leave your life of sin'" (John 8:10–11).

The woman was an adulteress. She was caught in her sin; clearly she was guilty. Jesus freed her from her sin. Forgiveness is the power to loose people from their sin. This power is given to the church, to be exercised in every believer.

When confronted with our sin, we must confess. When confession is made, we must forgive. But forgiveness is only the first step toward reconciliation. Accountability for our actions demands more, as we will see in our final chapter.

Notes

1. George MacDonald, *Thomas Wingfold, Curate* (Whitethorn, Calif.: Johannesen, 1996), 457. Originally published by Hurst & Blackett (London) in 1876.
2. L. Gregory Jones, *Embodying Forgiveness: A Theological Analysis* (Grand Rapids: Eerdmans, 1995), 44.
3. Dietrich Bonhoeffer, *Life Together* (San Francisco: Harper & Row, 1954), 131.

4. Ibid., 133–34.

5. Ibid., 47.

6. Read Scripture's call to "fight the good fight" and live into your good confession in the presence of many witnesses in 1 Timothy 6:12–13.

7. John Howard Yoder, "Binding and Loosing," *The Royal Priesthood* (Scottdale, Pa.: Herald, 1998), 335.

Thirteen

DISCIPLINE AND RESTITUTION:
HOW WE ARE RE-FORMED

Those whom I love I rebuke and discipline.
So be earnest, and repent.

     ~ REVELATION 3:19

Proper confession should lead to forgiveness. And that is our goal—to be forgiven, right? Wrong. Forgiveness is not reconciliation; it is barely the first step to being restored. Reconciliation is living together in the light of our confession and forgiveness. Reconciliation is a commitment to transformation.

Here again we are confronted with the difference between private religion and the community of Jesus Christ. The church calls us to be fully reconciled to God, our brothers and sisters, and to ourselves. As we noted earlier, the work of sin and darkness is to separate us in each of these relationships. The longer we spend in the dark, the harder it is to live—that is, stay—in the light. For reconciliation to fully restore the sinner to fellowship, it must change our character as well as forgive our sin.

God wants to do far more than forgive us; He wants to change us. All confession and forgiveness of sin is about character. All reconciliation requires confronting a history and redeeming habits formed and practiced over many years. These sinful patterns of thinking and acting are part of our character: habits that must be explored, owned, and reconstituted under the guidance of God's Word, His Spirit, and the community of believers.

Reconstituting character requires discipline and restitution. It is not enough to forgive a sinner. The church must come alongside to correct and encourage. The church must set and keep boundaries for accountability and growth. The church must encourage the sinner to demonstrate his good confession by paying back his debt of sin to those he has offended and hurt. The church must be the church.

Some Definitions

Both Greek and Hebrew words for *discipline* in Scripture refer to a kind of "chastening" or "correction" for the benefit of learning. The word is frequently linked in Proverbs to wisdom and knowledge.[1] Discipline is a pathway to growth and maturity. The Scriptures tell us:

> Endure hardship as discipline; God is treating you as sons. For what son is not disciplined by his father? If you are not disciplined (and everyone undergoes discipline), then you are illegitimate children and not true sons. Moreover, we have all had human fathers who disciplined us and we respected them for it. How much more should we submit to the Father of our spirits and live! . . . No discipline seems pleasant at the time, but painful. Later on, however, it produces a harvest of righteousness and peace for those who have been trained by it. (Hebrews 12:7–9, 11)

The *New International Version* of the Old Testament chooses to use the word *restitution* eighteen times as a translation for the Hebrew root word meaning "to be in a covenant of peace." To make restitution is to complete a payment, to make compensation. The word *restitution* never appears in the New Testament, but it is implied in various places. For instance, the apostle Paul wrote that a thief must not only stop stealing but get a job: "He who has been stealing must steal no longer, but must work, doing something useful with his own hands, that he may have something to share with those in need" (Ephesians 4:28). The one who steals must reconstitute his character, that is, replace habits of stealing with habits of work and generosity.

Discipline and restitution call the sinner to a changed life. This requires four traits:

1. Acceptance of need
2. Humility
3. Courage
4. Submission to a process of change under God's Word, the Holy Spirit, and God's community

A changed life also takes time. The greater history of the sin, the longer the reformation process will take.

The goal of God for discipline and restitution is always restoration. He desires that we be restored to Him. God allows conflict in order that we might see our darkness and seek out the light. He has called us into the church so that we might be confronted, corrected, and encouraged to change.

PRINCIPLES FOR DISCIPLINE AND RESTITUTION

But how does the church render discipline and restitution in a way that safeguards against legalism or shame? The following are four general principles for all church discipline and restitution:

1. BE GENTLE

Scripture teaches that discipline and restitution must be gentle. Paul wrote to the Galatians, "Brothers, if someone is caught in a sin, you who are spiritual should restore him gently. But watch yourself, or you also may be tempted" (Galatians 6:1). To be gentle is to be meek, trusting God's work in the sinner, not your will. Gentleness or meekness is the opposite of self-assertion and self-interest. We come alongside the sinner by the fruit of the Spirit. This is a yielding to God. It is practicing what Jesus said: "Take my yoke upon you and learn from me, for I am gentle and humble in heart, and you will find rest for your souls" (Matthew 11:29).

The aim of discipline is always a gentle restoration. It is never punishment or vindication; it's always intended to restore the brother or sister to fellowship. This is particularly relevant to the discipline of one whose sin has been against leadership. The apostle Paul told Timothy, "Those who oppose [the Lord's servant] he must gently instruct, in the hope that God will grant them repentance leading them to a knowledge of the truth" (2 Timothy 2:25). The leader's role is always to gently instruct. It is God's role to convict.

2. BE RELATIONAL

Discipline and restitution assume relationship. Paul instructed the Galatians to be gentle and caring; we are to "carry each other's burdens" (6:2). Furthermore, "We who are strong ought to bear with the failings of the weak and not to please ourselves" (Romans 15:1). Concerning our relationships with each other, Paul wrote:

> Therefore, as God's chosen people, holy and dearly loved, clothe yourselves with compassion, kindness, humility, gentleness and patience. Bear with each other and forgive whatever grievances you may have against one another. Forgive as the Lord forgave you. And over all these virtues put on love, which binds them all together in perfect unity.

Let the peace of Christ rule in your hearts, since as members of one body you were called to peace. And be thankful. Let the word of Christ dwell in you richly as you teach and admonish one another with all wisdom, and as you sing psalms, hymns and spiritual songs with gratitude in your hearts to God. And whatever you do, whether in word or deed, do it all in the name of the Lord Jesus, giving thanks to God the Father through him. (Colossians 3:12–17)

Our attitude toward the sinner must always be as a brother or sister, the Scriptures tell us. (See, for example, 2 Thessalonians 3:15.)

3. BE BENEFICIAL

Discipline and restitution are for the personal and corporate good. Discipline is always for good, never for harm. Those who administer discipline must never punish, shame, or embarrass. Discipline and restitution are the application of God's grace to heal and to change our character from sin to holiness. Remember the words of Paul:

When you were slaves to sin, you were free from the control of righteousness. What benefit did you reap at that time from the things you are now ashamed of? Those things result in death! But now that you have been set free from sin and have become slaves to God, the benefit you reap leads to holiness, and the result is eternal life. (Romans 6:20–22)

4. BE PURPOSEFUL

Finally, discipline and restitution must be purposeful. The purpose of discipline and restitution is restoration. The sinner is restored to God in worship, to others in shared life and peace, and to self in changed character. The purpose of discipline and restitution is peace in Christ.

DISCIPLINE IN ACTION

Every situation requiring discipline or restitution is complex and unique. It is the task of leaders to discern what is appropriate for the person and sin involved. Beware of stock methods or remedies for changing character.

Church leaders must use the principles above to craft a pathway of accountability and change, based upon the history of the sinner and the sin. For instance, people with addictive behaviors often require strict boundaries and accountability. People with destructive or abusive attitudes toward women or children must be kept from hurting others in the church. It is the responsibility of leadership to provide boundaries that guide the sinner and protect the flock.

Doug was physically abusive to his wife and children. This was well known in the church but never confronted before we arrived. When we observed his behavior, we scheduled an appointment to talk with Doug and his wife.

We asked Doug a lot of questions about how he treated his family and why. Doug told us about growing up in a very abusive family. He admitted that he had always had a problem with anger; he had no other skills and knew no other way. Doug minimized his actions. We explored with Doug his responsibility before God to love his wife and care for his children. Doug knew what was required but claimed he had tried to change for years and always failed.

We asked Doug if he wanted to change and if he would submit to a process of discipline and restitution. Doug agreed. The church removed Doug from his home and arranged for him to live with another family in the church who were mature and did not have kids in the home.

We asked Doug to submit to a process of working through the issues in his life that led to his abusive behavior. He signed a covenant outlining our agreement. The covenant spoke of our commitment as a church to come alongside Doug. Specifically, the elders and spiritual leaders would lead a moral and pure life; they would pray for Doug daily and meet with him weekly. The covenant spelled out Doug's commitment to do several things as well: meet with the pastor and elders weekly, receive counseling alone and with his wife, and work on several issues pertinent to his character. Doug also agreed that he would not go home without permission or without escort from a church leader. We welcomed Doug to attend church, but he could not take Communion or speak publicly in a service.

At the same time, the church leaders would come alongside Doug's wife, making arrangements for her to meet regularly with a Christian counselor and two mature women in the church. All counselors and each participant agreed to work together under the authority of the church.

On the Sunday following our confrontation we dismissed visitors after the morning service and announced to members the discipline covenant with Doug. We told the congregation what everyone already knew—that the marriage was "broken" and the elders were intervening. We did not give details but announced the decisions made. "We want you to know that the elders are aware of the issue and are addressing it directly," we said. "We ask you to allow the elders to be elders. We ask you to pray for us and to love Doug, his wife, and the family. We are giving you permission to lovingly discuss this with one another and with your brother, but not to gossip, and not to worry about what's happening. We will report to you when there is more to say."

We met with Doug each week for several months. As long as Doug was making an effort, grace was being applied.

The elders explored ways that Doug could make restitution to his wife, family, and the church. This included paying for a daughter's dance lessons he had denied before, providing for his wife to visit relatives out of state, and giving professional services to the church. All of these were announced and explained to church members.

The Hard Work of Reconciliation

The final chapter in Doug's life is still being written. He has the opportunity to continue walking into the light or to resign himself to darkness. It is for the church to warn, to love, and to discern.

We have used a similar process outlined above with three other men whose sin varied from addiction to pornography and adultery. Each man submitted to months of structured accountability, counseling, and acts of restitution. Each was restored to his marriage and to fellowship in the church.

Not all efforts at reconciliation end well. Reconciliation is hard work, demanding perseverance and faith to continually walk into the light. We have been shocked and saddened by some who choose the darkness and refuse the light. But we have seen God move in amazing power to redeem those who will submit to a process of redemption.

Reconciliation is a long walk no believer can make alone. It is living by faith in a disciplined community under God's Word and Spirit.

Overcoming church conflict means seeing beyond sin and forgiveness to claim a life shaped by a kingdom yet to come. Keep in mind what the apostle John saw and wrote about, a kingdom where sin and strife are finally banished forever:

Then I saw a new heaven and a new earth, for the first heaven and the first earth had passed away, and there was no longer any sea. I saw the Holy City, the new Jerusalem, coming down out of heaven from God, prepared as a bride beautifully dressed for her husband. And I heard a loud voice from the throne saying, "Now the dwelling of God is with men, and he will live with them. They will be his people, and God himself will be with them and be their God. He will wipe every tear from their eyes. There will be no more death or mourning or crying or pain, for the old order of things has passed away." He who was seated on the throne said, "I am making everything new!" . . .

"He who overcomes will inherit all this, and I will be his God and he will be my son." (Revelation 21:1–5, 7)

THE MARVEL OF RESTORATION

In Florence, Italy, stands the majestic, twenty-five-foot marble statue of David. For Michelangelo, sculpting was the act of discovery, not invention. An inventor would have approached the stone to see what he could make. Michelangelo, on the other hand, began with the assumption that David was already in the stone before he touched it. His job was to uncover the figure that was already there. Michelangelo carved the stone by taking away everything that was not David.

Restoration is taking away everything that is not Christ. David, the shepherd who became the king of Israel, is a good model of restoration. Though loved and blessed of God, David sinned grievously as king. His adulterous affair with Bathsheba and subsequent murder of Uriah are among the most grievous sins in recorded history.

When the prophet Nathan confronted David with his sin, declaring, "You are the man!" (2 Samuel 12:7), the king fell to his knees and repented. "I have sinned against the Lord," he said (v. 13). David bore the heavy price and consequences of his sin. Psalm 51 records David's confession, plea for restoration, and promise of restitution:

Create in me a pure heart, O God, and renew a steadfast spirit within me. Do not cast me from your presence or take your Holy Spirit from me. Restore to me the joy of your salvation and grant me a willing spirit, to sustain me. Then I will teach transgressors your ways, and sinners will turn back to you. (10 –14)

Found in darkness, David turned immediately to the light and was restored.

In Italy, circling David's statue, are many other figures. These are statues of slaves that Michelangelo carved with crude and contorted faces. Only the top and mid-section of each slave's torso is carved. Michelangelo left the bottom block of marble untouched, the figures enslaved in stone.

Michelangelo helps us picture what the apostle Paul wrote to the Galatians, that need to break free from our sins: "It is for freedom that Christ has set us free. Stand firm, then, and do not let yourselves be burdened again by a yoke of slavery" (Galatians 5:1).

God knew you, like David, before the creation of the world. He called you out of darkness and slavery into freedom and light. You were like a slave trapped in stone. God has set you free.

Reconciliation is not invention. It's not conforming to a set of laws or methods. It is not working more, trying harder, or being better. Instead, it is the spiritual work of God, chipping away everything in you that is not Christ.

Scripture reminds us that sin makes discipline necessary, and discipline makes restoration possible. Indeed, discipline is a sign of God's love for us as His children—God's loving, healing remedy for those who wander away from the light.

A church that disciplines in love for gentle restoration will be a church that makes peace.

Note

1. Proverbs 1:2–3, 7; 5:12 ,23; 6:23; 10:17; 12:1; 13:18; 15:5, 10, 32; 22:15; 23:12–13, 23.

EPILOGUE:
SEVEN CALLS TO REPENTANCE

Imagine that you are a leader of a church practicing biblical, one-another community. You're married, and like all Christian spouses, you struggle at times with issues and disagreements with your mate. But in your church it is safe to reveal your struggles and to ask for help.

In fact, every year on your anniversary, your wife (or husband) and you invite to your home about twenty Christian brothers and sisters. These friends, some married, some single, arrive to celebrate and grow your marriage; men gather with men in one room, women with women in another. For about forty minutes you talk about your marriage over the past, admitting your struggles, laughing at your foibles, and naming your failures. Your friends ask questions and offer observations, insights, and counsel. When a verse comes to mind, you read it together and reflect on its truth. When a specific need is mentioned, you stop and pray.

As the time of sharing and reflection comes to an end, everyone gathers together in a larger room to discuss what was learned and discerned. You offer confession to your spouse in front of your friends, then make specific commitments to your partner that you desire to fulfill, inviting these friends to keep you accountable. Your spouse does the same. You renew your vows of love and fidelity for the year ahead.

The evening ends with your spouse and you sitting in the middle of the room as your friends encircle you, place hands on you, and pray for your health and protection as they commit your next year of marriage to the Lord.

Can you imagine such a scene? Can you envision what this would do for your marriage and your church? How many marriages (and ministers) could be saved and conflicts prevented if we practiced simple rituals like this, which remind us of our faith and rehearse our commitment?

Peace is the fruit of God's Spirit formed in biblical community. Making peace is the result of God's people being claimed by and putting into practice the Gospel story.

Reconciliation is a way of life that claims our personal and private lives; it will affect our marriages and our single lives, the way we raise children and express our fellowship. It will affect how we worship. The church just after Pentecost was comprised of people who constantly submitted to God's Word, His Spirit, and each other (see Acts 2). This is the fellowship that must be restored if the church is to be redemptive.

Yes, we are sinners, and the conflicts in our churches all trace their causes to our selfish choices. Yet Scripture calls us to be a redemptive community, and by seeking, first and foremost, the lordship of Christ, we can redeem our community.

For the church to be true peacemakers, we must repent, that is, change our ways. Here are seven calls to practice repentance in the church—repentance that brings change.

1. RECOVER COMMUNITY

We call the church to recover community: to renounce the widespread cultural syncretism of individualism and autonomy and to replace it with biblical, one-another community. The church must become a redemptive community where God inhabits His people; where God works in spatial ways to love, heal, forgive, encourage, and grow a community of believers. The church is the empowering presence of the Holy Spirit guiding a people to be the active, present witness of a future reality.[1]

2. RESTORE HOLINESS

We call the church to restore holiness: to be a holy place where God is actively transforming His people toward completion in Christ. The church must be a people of character, the social construction of a spiritual reality—salvation and sanctification in our midst. When it is, we will become a nurturing, vision-forming community of called-out, called-together people who embody truth.[2]

3. REVIVE SPIRITUAL GIFTS

We call the church to revive, exercise, and affirm the authority of spiritual gifts, every member serving by the gifting of the Holy Spirit according to his "measure of faith." We affirm the church as the body of Christ, with all members called and gifted to serve.[3]

4. RENEW CONFESSION

We call the church to be a confessional community: to be a community of forgiven saints gathered around a common confession of sin and the redeeming work of Jesus Christ. By confessing sin, the truthfulness of forgiveness becomes manifest; in proclaiming Christ, we describe a specific kind of people, separated unto Christ, living in a world formed by the power of His resurrection. In confession, the church embodies a living, sustaining reality, a commitment to a specific way, truth, and life.[4]

5. Reclaim Scripture

We call the church to return Scripture to its rightful place as the historical, life-giving description of what it means to follow Christ truthfully. The church must release Scripture from the excess of right-handed, purely objective propositional and left-handed, subjective experiential interpretation.

- From the propositional, in which Scripture is a prescriptive rule book of dos and don'ts, and Christianity is reduced to the sum of what we "know."

- From the experiential, in which Scripture becomes a place where individuals project their subjective experience into the text for personal interpretation, and Christianity is reduced to what we "feel."

We call the church to reclaim Scripture as the transforming revelation of God's salvation history, where truth and rightful authority are borne out in a way of life. Scripture offers a new reality based upon the specific history of God's called-out people, who not merely "know, do, and feel" but "become" a people transformed by the power and wisdom of the resurrected Christ.[5]

6. Reestablish Witness

We call the church to be a living witness to the world of the life-changing resurrection of Jesus Christ. We call the church to be a people truly separate, demonstrating salvation, justification, and sanctification as a life journey, not an event alone; a way of life, not a status achieved. We call the church to "life-space evangelism," to put salvation on display through the active life and authentic word of distinctly Christian character and community.[6]

7. REDEFINE LEADERSHIP

We call the church to redefine the role of leadership according to the Spirit's call, gifting, and authority affirmed by the body rather than achieved by vocation, education, or election. We call the church to recognize the boundaries of pastor and leader roles and to encourage service by spiritual gifting and interdependent, collaborative teams rather than autocratic fiat or democratic autonomy.[7]

Notes

1. Scripture's many commands for this active, present witness of a future reality include Romans 12:10, 16; 13:8; 14:13; 15:7, 14; 16; 1 Corinthians 1:10; Galatians 5:13; Ephesians 4:2, 32; 5:19, 21. There are many others.
2. Matthew 5:48; Ephesians 5:25–27; Philippians 1:9–11.
3. 1 Corinthians 12:4–7; 27; Romans 12:3–6.
4. Hebrews 13:15; James 5:16; 1 John 1:9.
5. Romans 12:1–2; 2 Timothy 3:14–4:2.
6. Acts 2:42–48; 1 Thessalonians 1:6–10.
7. The relationships and boundaries among leaders as well as the interdependent relationships within the body are displayed in the apostle Paul's final greetings and admonishment to the Romans; see Romans 16:1–17; 21–23. See also 1 Corinthians 6:1; Philippians 4:3; Colossians 4:11; Philemon 23–24.

APPENDIX:
FORMING A SAFE PLACE GROUP

After beginning with the Spirit, are you now trying to attain your goal by human effort?

— GALATIANS 3:3

Metanoia Ministries and the author recommend that churches form "safe place" groups among their leaders to foster accountability, awareness, and action regarding conflict in the church. The eight elements of a safe place group were briefly introduced in chapter 11. Here are the specific steps for forming and maintaining a safe place group. Much of the material that follows has been adapted from mutual conversations and practice with my friend David Fitch, Ph.D. Dr. Fitch has implemented the program in several men's and women's accountability groups.

— Prayer. This is the practice of submitting our complete lives to the lordship of Christ and His work in us. Begin and end each gathering with prayer, inviting the Spirit's presence for discernment of truth and to seal the work of God in the believer's life.

~ Check-in. Each person's check-in should be a concise description of where they are emotionally, which influences the dynamics of the group. Determine what basic emotion the person feels: mad, glad, sad, afraid, or ashamed. Each person is asked to speak truthfully, that is, with words that have integrity with his or her emotions and behavior. Following the check-in, the group may choose to explore the issues of one person, or a pattern of collective issues raised, more in depth. A facilitator should guide the meeting.

~ Repentance. Each person recognizes the role of repentance before the Cross. He comes to the group prepared to recognize when sin is present in his life, own it, accept the forgiveness of the Cross for it, and repent of it. To repent means more than to be sorry and accept forgiveness, but to make restitution, turn away, and look to God in Christ for His empowerment toward a new direction that may not be known or even possible yet.

~ Work. The term *work* refers to the process of submitting our lives to the work of the Spirit in and through the safe place group. This does not mean that it is up to each person to work hard to get at a solution. Rather, we submit to honest questions, searching our hearts and emotions, allowing the Spirit to seek out all truth; to "work" in the sense of "work out your salvation with fear and trembling" (Philippians 2:12).

~ Intervention. Each person grants permission, and invites participation of others in the group, to speak the truth in love into their circumstances, with care and noncoercion. Often this will concern a repeated pattern that needs recognition, accountability, and repentance.

~ Submission in trust. The unifying goal of the group is to form a community where all are committed to each other's growth and development in Christ. This requires trust and honesty. If anyone has enmity with another brother, he should make things right before the meeting, so as not to disrupt the meeting. Such trust is essential. The premise of the group is that each person submit to the Holy Spirit and to each other "in the Lord." Even when disagreements or injustices appear, the trust in the group is that the Holy Spirit will work in and through such instances for our good and that injustice will be met with righteousness eventually.

- Accountability. There are times in every person's life when he needs to specifically develop new habits with the help of the Holy Spirit and the community in order to overcome sin. Such an accountability structure is an important practice. Most often this practice requires a commitment to partner with someone who will check in once a week over the phone with a given list of questions.

- Speaking into a person's life. There will come a time in every believer's work when it may be appropriate to speak into a brother's life with a verse of Scripture, an understanding of God, a story for enlightenment, or a clarification of a perspective as seen from the Christian's point of view. This occurs in a conversational, noncoercive fashion, usually after a time of confession when a person locates an emotion, uncovers what is beneath it, and arrives at a confession. At this time, it may be appropriate for one to engage the person, using spiritual gifts in submission to the Spirit. Phrases that may be useful in approaching the brother include "Can I speak something to you into this situation?" and "Here's a verse of Scripture that may say something to you in this."

- Contributing to the group. Each member may contribute and speak freely. Be sensitive. Speak out of a sensitivity to the Holy Spirit in accordance with faith measured out to you in the Holy Spirit. Take risks. Test out your intuition. If you are not acting as a "point person," then feed your input to whoever is doing that. Too many voices can become confusing to the person working.

With these elements in place, the group should run effectively, though at times there may be tensions and certainly disagreements. Yet there may come a time when one person is so at odds with the purposes of this group and continually chooses to work against the purposes of this group that he or she may be asked to leave. Is there ever an occasion to expel a group member? Yes; when the group unanimously agrees that they cannot enable this person in an area of sin.

Requesting the individual to leave the group should take place only for the sake of the group's and the individual's welfare. There is a time when the "working out" of that brother's (or sister's) own salvation in Christ is best served by being apart from the group.